The Impact of Graded Tests

The Impact of
Graded Tests

David Pennycuick and Roger Murphy

 The Falmer Press

(A member of the Taylor & Francis Group)
London, New York and Philadelphia

UK The Falmer Press, Falmer House, Barcombe, Lewes, East Sussex, BN8 5DL

USA The Falmer Press, Taylor & Francis Inc., 242 Cherry Street, Philadelphia, PA 19106-1906

Copyright © D. Pennycuick and R. Murphy 1988

First published in 1988

British Library Cataloguing in Publication Data

Pennycuick, David
 The impact of graded tests.
 1. Examinations—Great Britain.
 2. Grading and marking (Students).
 2. Education, Secondary—Great Britain.
 I. Title. II. Murphy, Roger.
 373.12′6 LB3056.G7.

ISBN 1-85000-277-0
ISBN 1-85000-278-9 (Pbk.)

Library of Congress Cataloging-in-Publication Data

Pennycuick, David
 The impact of graded tests/David Pennycuick and
Roger Murphy.
  p. cm.
 Bibliography: p.
 Includes index.
 1. High schools—Great Britain—Examinations. 2. Grading and marking (Students)—Great Britain.
 I. Murphy, Roger. II. Title.
LB3060.26.P46 1988 373.12′7′0941—dc19
ISBN 1-85000-277-0
ISBN 1-85000-278-9 (Pbk.)

Typeset in 11/13 Bembo by
Alresford Typesetting & Design, New Farm Road, Alresford, Hants.

Printed in Great Britain by Taylor & Francis (Printers) Ltd, Basingstoke

Contents

Preface

This book is based on David Pennycuick's Ph.D. research, which was conducted in the Assessment and Examinations Unit of Southampton University Department of Education, and supervised by Roger Murphy. Chapter 1 sets the background for the research, and describes general features of graded tests and graded assessment. The research evidence, which is mainly in the form of case study data on three selected graded test schemes but also includes information about a range of other schemes, is presented in Chapters 2, 3 and 4. The following two chapters are devoted to analysis of this evidence, and focus on the impact of graded tests on teaching, learning and assessment. Finally, Chapter 7 is concerned with the relationship of graded tests to other current assessment developments, including records of achievement, GCSE, and tests associated with the proposed National Curriculum.

The research programme was supported by an Economic and Social Research Council Collaborative Award Studentship, and by the Southern Regional Examinations Board. It also depended on the cooperation and goodwill of many other organizations and their staff, but especially the four local education authorities and the schools in which the fieldwork was carried out. The authors are grateful to the advisers, headteachers, staff, pupils and other individuals who agreed to be interviewed, and we are indebted to our colleagues at Southampton for many stimulating discussions. In particular, we should like to express our thanks to Harry Torrance, John Evans, Diane Fairbairn and Henry Macintosh.

Chapter 1

Introduction

The Debate about Assessment in Secondary Schools

How pupils are assessed in secondary schools in Britain is, has been, and will no doubt remain an issue of great interest for both the general public and those with a professional responsibility for, or involvement in, this part of the education system. The reasons for this are numerous and in most cases fairly apparent. For example it is widely recognized that assessment procedures have a strong influence on both how the curriculum is taught and how pupils approach their study of it. It is also fairly commonly asserted that the curriculum in primary schools, and in further and higher education, are in turn influenced to a considerable extent by the assessments and examinations carried out in secondary schooling (Hargreaves, 1982). Assessments tend to define what is understood by achievement, and therefore influence what happens before and after they occur.

Another major role that assessment systems perform in secondary schools is in relation to selection for further education and employment. Broadfoot (1979 and 1984) among others has pointed to this social control function of public examinations as one of the major reasons for their continued existence. The great attraction of public examinations for 16 year olds is that they are perceived by many as providing relatively straightforward information about achievement, and the results are based on a system that is thought to be relatively fair and free from major sources of bias or error.

Surveys of employers and others who use examination results as part of their selection procedures (Jones, 1984) reveal that in general the results are not seen as conveying anything very specific in terms of levels of achievement in relation to particular aspects of the curriculum, but are used more as a general sieve, before more detailed selection procedures are applied to those applicants who survive the initial part of the selection process.

Without at this stage reviewing all the arguments for and against public examinations, it quickly becomes apparent that what is being looked for in assessment procedures in secondary schools depends upon which of a number of issues are seen as having the greatest priority. Employers and selectors, it may be argued, are happiest with traditional end-of-course public examinations because they yield results which are easy to interpret and use. Many professional educators on the other hand are concerned by the influence that such examinations have on the secondary-school curriculum and the way in which it is taught in schools around the country. Added to these concerns is the growing fear that with the raising of the school-leaving age to 16, public examinations have failed to cater for the entire age cohort that is still in school at this stage. It has been widely argued (Burgess and Adams, 1980; Mortimore and Mortimore, 1984) that public examinations at 16+ have a major influence in distorting the curriculum and pupils' perceptions of successful achievement in comprehensive schools in such a way that a large proportion of secondary-school children become disillusioned and leave school with a general sense of alienation and failure.

It is interesting in this respect that following a major review of secondary schooling and the causes of underachievement in the ILEA, reported in the Hargreaves Report (ILEA, 1984), assessment was singled out as one of, if not the, major factor in contributing to underachievement. In that report it is argued that public examinations have led to far too narrow a definition of achievement, and have provided far too distant and remote a target for many pupils to work towards. One of the suggested strategies to deal with this problem is to break the curriculum up into smaller units and assess the various aspects of the achievements of pupils as they study these units, rather than at a fixed point of time at the end of a two-, three- or four-year course.

The idea of working towards short-term goals, where the levels of achievement expected are widely understood by pupils and teachers, is central to the development work on units and unit credits that is now going on in ILEA schools. Similar developments are to be found in other parts of the country where many schools are developing modules and assessment arrangements that can operate within a modular curriculum framework. All of these developments may be seen to have a relationship, in part at least, to the work on graded assessments and tests which is the focus for this book.

A major distinction between graded tests and more recent developments in relation to units and modules is a curricular one, in that graded tests in most cases have been developed within a traditional separate individual subject approach to the curriculum. In contrast, units and modules may either be themselves cross-curricular, or promote greater breaking down of subject boundaries in the routes through the overall curriculum that are opened up by them.

In terms of the assessment approaches represented by these related developments there is potentially much more in common. The move has in many cases been away from formal end-of-course exams, say after two or three years, towards much more immediate assessments either during or at the conclusion of much shorter periods of study, in relation to the contents of each particular unit, module or set of graded objectives. In many cases this has led to an enhancement of the assessment responsibilities of individual teachers in weighing up the achievements of individual children against the stated criteria for success. Sometimes teachers at this stage are acting also as assessors, by certifying whether or not a pupil has reached the required levels of achievement; in other cases their role is to decide whether the pupil is ready to take a test which will ascertain whether or not the appropriate level of achievement or mastery has been reached.

Graded Tests and Graded Assessments

Although this book is primarily about developments within the 'graded test' movement, much of what is said can also be applied to 'graded assessment' schemes. In some cases these terms have been used interchangeably but a variety of reasons have also been put forward for preferring the broader 'graded assessment' approach. As yet few graded assessment (as opposed to graded test) schemes are fully operational, but one example is the East Midlands GOML* scheme. This scheme does not set common tests, but lays down assessment procedures.

Sometimes the distinction between 'assessment' and 'tests' may be made to draw attention to the continuous nature of the former, even where assessment is based solely on a sequence of tests. Some developers might argue alternatively that the word 'tests' should be avoided since it carries undesirable connotations of norm-referencing and psychometrics. Nuttall and Goldstein (1984) refer to possibly restrictive backwash effects of testing.

> One way to guard against the worst sort of backwash is to ensure that the assessment procedures validly measure the full diversity of curricular objectives. That requirement almost certainly demands an impressive array of oral, practical and written assessments, as well as course work, projects and other extended exercises so that we should talk of graded assessments rather than graded tests (Nuttall and Goldstein, 1984, p. 12).

*Graded Objectives in Modern Languages. See Chapter 2.

Harrison also considers backwash, and argues that 'the precept which seems to offer most hope for the integrity of graded assessments as a stimulator (rather than an inhibitor) of the curriculum is that it should be grounded firmly on best practice in the classroom' (p. 4). In emphasizing integration of teaching and learning with assessment, he adopts a slightly different perspective on the test/assessment distinction.

> The idea of testing being imposed from outside (a sorting procedure devised by Them) gives way to the idea of testing as a source of feedback to both learner and teacher on how well the course is going (a cooperative exercise between Us). Assessment therefore becomes the whole process of judging, including the mechanism for achieving the judgment, rather than merely the mechanism, the tests (Harrison, 1985, p. 2).

This suggests the question of whether it is possible for graded assessment schemes to incorporate mechanisms for the judgment process other than tests. One of the schemes currently under development which is attempting to do so is GAIM (Graded Assessment in Mathematics), in which a distinction is made between 'incidental' and 'purposive' assessment.

> The preferred method of assessment would be *incidental assessment*. This would take place when a teacher, while in discussion with a student or observing the student's work, noted that the student had, in fact, demonstrated competence in a particular criterion . . . It is however unlikely that all the criteria could be covered in this way and hence there is likely to be a need for *purposive assessment*, i.e. when a teacher sets a particular activity for a student or group of students with the aim of relating their performance to a particular criterion (GAIM, 1985, p. 26).

The concept of assessment here is far removed from traditional forms of test, although if we define tests to be predetermined and administered forms of assessment, there is a relation at least with the GAIM notion of purposive assessment. It remains to be seen whether the notion of incidental assessment can be successfully realized in practice, or whether schemes such as GAIM will find themselves forced to revert to more formal assessment styles in order to retain credibility for purposes of certification, particularly at higher levels. It is difficult to predict how important the test/assessment distinction will prove to be, and worth pointing out that in a recent review of oral/aural graded tests in modern languages Utley, Mitchell and Phillips (1983) make no distinction, defining assessment simply as 'testing'. This is an issue we will return to in Chapter 7 when we shall attempt to review the progress that has been made in the graded test schemes and speculate about the way in which graded tests and assessments may develop in the future.

Much of the focus of our attention in this book will not however be on the graded tests themselves, in terms for instance of their particular qualities as instruments of educational measurement, but will be on the impact such tests have had on teaching and learning, and classroom and school organization in a number of case-study schools, which were studied between 1984 and 1986.

As a first stage in this research process we were keen to arrive at a clearer definition than appeared to exist for what could count as a graded test scheme. In the next section we will explain in some detail the definition we arrived at, and the reasons why we chose this particular definition.

Characteristics of graded test schemes

The schemes to be considered vary in several important respects but have certain key features in common. The purpose of this section is to identify those features and to present a working definition of graded tests, although several aspects of this definition will require further clarification in subsequent sections. Variation among schemes is as follows:

(a) *Target group* Schemes are usually age-independent for candidature, but each scheme is nevertheless designed with a particular age and/or ability group in mind. Some schemes are aimed particularly or specifically at low-attaining pupils.

(b) *Syllabus* Apart from subject-specific characteristics, schemes differ in the extent to which they are associated with curriculum reform, and the nature of such reform; also in the extent to which scheme syllabuses are regarded as spanning the subject curriculum in respect of both content and process. Within a subject, graded test syllabuses may also vary both in approach to the subject and in presentation.

(c) *Pedagogy* Learning and testing are individualized to some extent in all schemes, but there are differences in the manner and the degree to which this occurs. Possible teaching styles may vary from class exposition to individual tuition, and from heuristic to didactic; some schemes may permit a range of approaches.

(d) *Assessment* There is a rich variety of assessment procedures and assessment styles (e.g. oral, practical, written).

(e) *Levels* There is no consistent pattern in the number or average frequency of available levels. Sometimes levels are subdivided, either in stages or in terms of results awarded. Most, but not all, schemes issue certificates to successful candidates.

(f) *Teacher involvement* The degree to which teachers are involved in syllabus and test design, in setting standards, and in test administration, is dependent on the scheme.

There is also variation among schemes in the relative emphasis given by developers and users of the schemes to the possible *functions* of graded tests, for example:

- to enhance pupil and/or teacher motivation, intrinsically and/or extrinsically;
- to act as a catalyst and vehicle for curricular and/or pedagogical reform;
- to provide a clear description of pupil attainment for purposes of certification, qualification, selection and guidance;
- to provide feedback on curricular and pedagogical effectiveness.
- to provide information for diagnosis and remediation of individual difficulties;
- to exert control over curriculum content, methods and standards;
- to monitor standards for purposes of accountability.

Some functions may not apply to particular graded test schemes, and others may be applicable but unintended by the scheme progenitors. All the functions also apply to methods of assessment other than graded testing, and although being important in consideration of the impact of schemes, they are of only limited value in an attempt to define the graded test concept.

Harrison (1982) takes a definition based on GOML schemes as a starting point. He argues that

a graded test scheme is progressive, with short-term objectives leading on from one to the next; that it is task-oriented, relating to the use of language for practical purposes; and that it is closely linked into the learning process, with pupils or students taking the tests when they are ready to pass (Harrison, 1982, p. 13).

Later, he explains that

The special meaning to be attached to the word 'task' in the context of graded tests is the application of what has been learnt to achieving some end rather than using it for the completion of testing exercises, which show only that knowledge or skill has been acquired (Harrison, 1982, p. 24).

Although many graded test items would satisfy this meaning of 'task', some would not (for example certain exercises in mathematics or music). Thus the assessment of applicable tasks may be regarded as a curricular aim of many adherents of graded tests, rather than as being essential to the graded test concept. On the other hand, Harrison's first condition, of progression, is satisfied by all of the schemes we have looked at, and is included in other definitions (for example Mortimore, 1983; Margaret Brown, 1983). It is therefore taken as the basis of our first key feature of graded tests.

Key feature A: level-progression
In a graded test scheme, there is a sequence of tests at progressive levels of difficulty, complexity, sophistication and/or syllabus content.

Within the subject matter of a scheme the learning process is analysed and organized into a series of stages, in most cases so that each stage builds on previous levels. It may be that such analysis is simpler in pyramidal sub-jects (for example, mathematics), where progression is clear, than in subjects such as history, which Harrison (1982) refers to as 'areas' subjects. In all sub-jects, however, sequencing decisions resulting in a hierarchy of levels are to some extent arbitrary, although in practice account will be taken of natural content or process sequences leading to convenient units of work which provide suitable short-term goals. Experience allows levels of difficulty of exercises or tasks to be assessed, and allocation to appropriate scheme levels to be carried out. It is not necessary for every pupil to follow the pro-gression absolutely, and there is often scope for flexibility in the order of treatment of topics within a level. As far as testing is concerned, certain levels may be bypassed, particularly if the scheme is arranged in such a way that each level and its associated tests subsume previous levels. In some cases (for example, in physical education) the same test item may be used for con-secutive levels, the progression being in terms of improved performance.

All graded test schemes are designed to enable pupils to progress through the levels over a substantial period of time. An example of an assess-ment system which is *not* progressive in this sense is the General Certificate of Secondary Education. In GCSE pupils are awarded one of a series of available grades to be recorded on a single certificate, rather than a series of certificates for successive grades (Harrison, 1982). In a graded test scheme 'graded' refers to the tests themselves, not to pupil performance on the tests. However, as Harrison points out, this distinction is not clear-cut; there are schemes (for example, music) which do distinguish between two or three degrees of successful candidate performance within a level, or 'grade'.

Harrison's definition refers to candidates taking the tests when they are ready to pass. Schemes typically, or at least ideally, have high pass rates, and this emphasis on success is characteristic of graded tests.

Key feature B: success-orientation
Graded tests are designed to be taken by students only when they have a high probability of success.

This principle that pupils take tests only when they are ready for them, and are therefore likely to succeed, perhaps can not always be realized in practice. However, success is *intended* for all, or almost all, pupils, and this is a genuine possibility in the sense that the level of achievement required for a pass is pre-determined, and independent of the performance of other pupils. There is no attempt to spread candidates out in a normal distribution, and each test is non-competitive. Those pupils who do fail can be given an opportunity for repetition of the test. Another aspect of the emphasis on success is the principle that pupils are tested on what they can rather than what they cannot do.

The link between success and motivation is stressed by Mortimore (1983).

> Graded tests could allow many more pupils to achieve some success and to be spared the scarring effects of failure that so inhibit motivation for further study. The avoidance of unnecessary failure may, in turn, trigger the potential for success in a higher pro-portion of pupils than at present. Assessment would then play its proper part in the educational process by *facilitating* rather than *inhibiting* effective learning (Mortimore, 1983, p. 10).

It is intended that pupils will be well-motivated by a feeling of achieve-ment after success at one level, and encouraged to aim for the next, which will not be too far ahead. There is also the interesting possibility that the short-term goals provided by graded test schemes may extend success and motivation at school to working-class pupils, for whom deferred grati-fication may be unacceptable (see ILEA, 1984).

The final aspect of Harrison's definition is that graded tests are 'closely linked into the learning process', and this leads to our third and final key feature.

Key feature C: curriculum-linking
Each graded test is closely linked to the curriculum for the relevant level by means of clear specification of the knowledge and processes to be assessed and of the standards to be attained.

Harrison (1982) states that 'One of the fundamental principles of the graded test approach is that it provides new and helpful ways of specifying exactly what will be taught and tested' (p. 20). Specification of knowledge and processes may be achieved by expressing objectives in behavioural terms on the syllabus, and perhaps listing them on certificates. In the case of written tests, specimen test items may be provided. Where tests are oral or practical the 'tasks' (in Harrison's sense) may be described in detail. Clear specification may be designed primarily for teachers, for certificate users, or for the pupils themselves. There is no intention to set questions which catch the candidate out, but instead graded tests are designed to enable candidates to demonstrate the knowledge and skills which they have learnt. The tests are such as to reflect pupils' classroom learning experiences accurately and fairly. Pupils can be given clear advance information about the skills and standards required, so that they know more or less what to expect. If standards are defined in terms of an aggregate mark, this can also be stated on the certificates together with the description of what successful candidates can do. Graded tests essentially test cognitive and/or psychomotor skills, not affective skills, and are tests of achievement, not aptitude.

Frequency of testing, and the spreading of testing through the course, are other factors enabling graded tests to be closely linked into the learning process. A further element in some schemes is the diagnostic use of test results to influence the teaching programme. Margaret Brown (1983) points out that 'the closeness of the relationship between curriculum organisation and assessment clearly varies considerably depending on the model of graded test system under consideration' (p. 6). In her view, 'the ultimate step in integration between curriculum and assessment is probably an individualised curriculum system of a graded nature' (p. 7). At the other extreme, intelligence tests would provide an example in which there is little or no link with the curriculum. Margaret Brown (1983) also points out the danger in curriculum-linking that the test system may become a 'curriculum tyrant', and notes 'a tendency of the graded test system to dictate the whole 13–16 or 11–16 curriculum for all children, which it would be capable of doing to a much greater degree than the present terminal examination' (p. 5).

Combining the three key features leads to our definition of graded tests, which is similar to, but expands upon, that given by Harrison (1982).

Definition In a graded test scheme, there is a sequence of tests at progressive levels of difficulty, complexity, sophistication and/or syllabus content, which are designed to be taken by students only when they have a high probability of success. Each test is closely linked to the curriculum for the relevant level by means of clear specification of the knowledge and processes to be assessed and of the standards to be attained.

More succinctly, graded tests are level-progressive, success-oriented and curriculum-linked. Different graded test models are possible (three are studied in detail in Chapters 2, 3 and 4) and in some cases theory may be overtaken by practical considerations. Thus implementation of the three key features may not be straightforward. Certainly a pragmatic approach to curriculum and assessment seems endemic in the graded test movement. This is one of the reasons why there is no reference to 'mastery learning' or to 'criterion-referencing' in our definition, although one or both are specified in other descriptions of graded tests (Freedman, 1982; London Regional Examining Board, 1982; Margaret Brown, 1983; Mortimore, 1983).

Both terms are also used by Harrison (1982). 'GOML tests form a progressive system of short-term goals based on a mastery-learning philosophy which should predicate criterion-referenced assessments resulting in success for nearly all candidates' (p. 30). However, Harrison found that the principles of criterion-referenced assessment are not strictly applied by GOML schemes in practice, and avoided the phrase 'criterion-referenced' in his working hypothesis. Utley, Mitchell and Phillips argue that 'in the end the important point may not be whether oral/aural tests *are* completely criterion-referenced, but how the concept has been used to help them evolve' (1983, p. 35).

Finally it may be noted that an earlier attempt to formulate a working definition (Pennycuick, 1983) included the requirement for graded tests to contain no options. Apart from general reliability problems created by the possibility that alternative items or sections may have differing facility levels, there is also the possibility that they may have differing taxonomic content (Willmott and Hall, 1975). In the specific context of graded tests, any significant inclusion of alternatives could lead to loss of clarity in the reporting of student attainment, and might also make a linear hierarchy of levels more difficult to define, while requiring more resources for the production of test items (Pennycuick, 1984). However, options can also provide greater syllabus flexibility, thus permitting choice for both teachers and candidates (Willmott and Hall, 1975; Tattersall, 1983). Indeed some schemes do include alternative items (for example, lists of set pieces in music exams) or optional sections (for example, a writing test in GOALS level 3). Thus the proposed condition for graded tests to contain no options, although desirable in some respects, is not sustained in practice, and in fact options did not emerge as a significant issue during the fieldwork.

The Search for Improved Assessment Systems

The interest in graded test schemes has occurred during a period where much attention in the British education system has been directed towards attempting to improve existing approaches to the assessment of pupils. In later chapters (2, 3 and 4) we will review in much more detail the specific graded test developments that have occurred in particular subjects. We will also, in Chapter 7, attempt to relate these developments to those that have occurred within profiling and records of achievement initiatives, and through the development of the new GCSE examination. At this stage we will just reflect a little further on some of the features of the graded test initiatives which have attracted particular attention in terms of meeting some of the desired characteristics of new assessment initiatives.

In an earlier review of various influential statements about the development of new curriculum and assessment initiatives (Murphy and Pennycuick, 1985) we summarized five features of assessment schemes that appeared to be common objectives for improvement. These features, which can be thought of as the qualities being looked for in new assessment initiatives were that such initiatives should:

1. record information about a *much wider range* of the achievements of pupils than have been emphasized through a narrow approach to educational assessment in the past;
2. lead to *meaningful* and positive descriptions of what *all* pupils can do;
3. *promote* rather than inhibit curriculum development and reform;
4. enhance pupil *motivation* and teacher morale and thus lead to an overall improvement in educational standards;
5. lead to a more *harmonious* relationship between assessment methods, curriculum design and teaching methods within individual schools (Murphy and Pennycuick, 1985, p. 2).

The extent to which any new scheme for pupil assessment can claim to meet these five objectives is bound to be open to debate. It is however possible to argue that many graded test schemes share most if not all of these objectives at least in terms of the impact that their constructors were attempting to achieve. The extent to which they have achieved these perhaps idealistic objectives is one of the central questions to be addressed by the research. At this stage it is perhaps worth reflecting a little further on Objectives 2 and 4.

Objective 2 breaks down into two separate but related parts. In essence the first part refers to the extent to which assessment systems can produce information about *what* pupils have achieved, as opposed to information about how their achievements compare with those of their classmates. The other characteristic required to satisfy this objective is that such information can be provided for all pupils, and not just a particular group with either high levels, or low levels, of achievement. Graded test schemes have attempted to meet these requirements by defining a sequence of levels, each linked to a set of descriptions of what pupils need to be able to do to satisfy the assessment criteria for that level, and together spanning a wide range of pupil achievement in that subject. Thus the expectation is that all pupils should, in principle at least, be able to satisfy the requirements of at least one of the levels. Also, whichever level they reach, it should be clear to both themselves, and other interested parties, what they had to do to be credited with a satisfactory performance at that level.

Thus graded tests involve explicit assessment criteria, even though they do not in most cases meet the full characteristics for a system of criterion-referenced assessment. Also depending on how they are actually used in schools they do have the potential for meeting Objective 4 by allowing pupils to work towards attainable targets and protecting them from a sense of failure by only entering them for the test when they are actually ready to take it. Thus the intention is to enhance pupil motivation by providing attainable targets in a system that involves the concepts of readiness, mastery learning and non-competitive assessment. Again just how far operational schemes can live up to these ideals in practice is a matter to be addressed in later chapters.

The link between graded tests and the concepts of 'mastery learning' and 'criterion referencing', which have been so influential in the development of assessment schemes in the USA, has frequently been observed, by authors such as Mortimore and Mortimore (1984): 'Each grade is intended to cover a certain amount of knowledge up to a defined standard. Pupils can progress by the "mastery learning" of a grade at a time, and, together, the grades form a progressive sequence . . .' (p. 64).

Graded tests can also be seen to have the potential to meet many of the requirements of those who like Withers and Cornish (1984) have been attracted by systems of non-competitive assessment.

> Non-competitive assessment has as its basic concern that only the performance of a particular student is observed, and only his or her most recent performances. The student is not compared with the performance of the 'ideal' (or even the 'other') students, nor with the old, very outdated information as to 'aptitude' or 'past achievement' or 'potential' which earlier teachers may have registered on report cards or record sheets. This type of assessment has simply to

do with recording and reporting as accurately as the teacher can the precise nature of the student's performance (Withers and Cornish, 1984, p. 3).

Withers and Cornish (1984) reject the claim that criterion-referenced assessment is by its very nature non-competitive, since students may compare grades even when grading of performance is based on specified criteria rather than on norms. However this depends on how criterion-referenced assessment is used. In 'graded tests' it is the tests themselves that are graded, rather than student performance on the tests, and it is worth asking to what extent graded tests are non-competitive. Certainly they are designed so that pupils do not compete against each other, but against a pre-determined standard. It is intended that the great majority of candidates should succeed, and it is perfectly consistent for pupils to cooperate with the teacher, and with each other, so that success should be achieved by the greatest possible number. Success can be recognized by the award of a certificate listing the acquired skills, and it is not necessary to report a mark or a grade, and certainly not a rank order. However it is unrealistic to suppose that all students will progress at the same speed, or reach the same final level, and both these means of differentiating between students form possible bases for competition. We may no longer ask 'Who can do better at the test?', but in a graded test scheme we may still ask 'Who can be ready faster?' or 'Who can progress further?' Indeed graded test results may be used to provide guidance to students on whether to continue the study of a subject. Thus graded tests can be regarded as a move towards the ideals of Withers and Cornish (1984), but the extent to which they meet them depends a great deal on how they are perceived and used by pupils, teachers and parents in the schools that use them. This is another issue to which we will return.

The preceding paragraphs have highlighted some of the unanswered questions about graded tests, and their impact on teaching and learning in schools, which we set out to explore in the research study, which is reported in this book. They are, in our view, exciting questions because they are at the heart of the current debate about the relationship between the curriculum, pupil assessment and learning, the timetable and school organization. Thus we set out to study them with great interest, but at the same time reserving our judgment about what in practice we were likely to find.

We will now turn briefly to consider the nature of the research exercise and the methods of data collection that were used. As the research followed the pattern of other recent educational research studies, we will not provide very much in the way of a description or discussion of the methods used. However readers wishing to learn more about the methodology used are referred to a much fuller account of this aspect of the study in Pennycuick (1986).

The Focus for the Research Project

The research to be presented in the following chapters was focused specifically on three particular graded test schemes, which fell within our definition of a graded test, and which were being used in the eight case-study schools studied during a period between 1984 and 1986. These schemes were the West Sussex GOALS scheme in modern languages, the Kent Mathematics Project and the School Science Certificate, which was first developed in Avon and Wiltshire.

In each subject area the findings presented were based on research data collected through intensive case studies, in each of the schools, which involved a range of data collection techniques including the study of documents, semi-structured interviews with staff and pupils, and classroom observation. In each case various checks were built into the procedures to attempt to verify the findings, and at each stage every attempt was made to encourage informants and respondents to draw to our attention particular issues that were of concern to them. The checks on the data collected included returning interview transcripts to interviewed teachers, and returning school case study reports to individual schools. In a small number of cases minor revisions or corrections were suggested and these have been taken into account in the summary presentation of the data provided here.

In essence the research approach falls within the broad tradition of illuminative evaluation (Parlett and Hamilton, 1976). It was conducted on the basis of a number of condensed case studies (Walker, 1974), which were carried out on eight schools in the South of England. The schools were selected on the basis of representing a variety of types of secondary schools, serving a variety of catchment areas. They were all known to be using one of the three graded test schemes that we wished to study, and were able to grant access for up to two weeks' fieldwork.

The findings from these case studies will now be presented in each of the next three chapters. In each case these will be placed in the context of the wider movement towards the development of graded tests in modern languages, mathematics and other subjects. We will also be returning to some of the issues raised in this opening chapter in order to discuss them further in the light of the evidence collected in the case studies.

Chapter 2

Graded Tests in Modern Languages

The GOML Movement

It was in modern languages that the term 'graded tests' came into prominence, as a result of local initiatives by groups of secondary school teachers dissatisfied with traditional methods of teaching and examining. The first GOML (Graded Objectives in Modern Languages) schemes were established in Oxfordshire, York and Lothian, and in 1979, when there were twenty-eight schemes under development, a national GOML coordinating committee was set up, with support from CILT (the Centre for Information on Language Teaching and Research). By 1985 the number of GOML groups had reached eighty-eight (Page, 1985) with over 300 000 pupils involved, but Harrison (1982) points out that GOML schemes are all independent and autonomous, although they are based on similar aims and have many methodological principles in common.

There are two strands to the major reform of modern-language teaching brought about by the GOML movement, strands which are conceptually separate although linked in practice. One is the move towards a communicative approach to language learning, often associated with functional/notional syllabuses and the work of the Council of Europe (van Ek, 1977). The other strand, with which this book is primarily concerned and which is generalizable to other subject areas, is that of graded tests, which imply the provision of clearly defined objectives and progressive short-term goals, with the accent on pupil success. Assessment is seen as an integral part of the learning process, and in modern languages this has led to an emphasis on oral/aural testing, which is seen as essential for the communicative approach, in spite of various practical difficulties detailed by Utley, Mitchell and Phillips (1983). There has been an attempt to make test items authentic and relevant to the learners' communicative needs. Writing is not tested at lower levels of most schemes and when it is introduced it is usually restricted to letter-writing. In all testing, whether pupil responses are appropriate and understandable is more important than whether they are accurate. Although they may have particular advantages for low-ability learners, GOML schemes are not specifically aimed at this group, or indeed any particular ability group or age range, but are intended to be geared to individual progress. Certificates are awarded to successful candidates at each level, usually by the relevant LEA.

The GOML movement is still evolving, and notwithstanding commonality of purpose and approach, there are significant variations in syllabus design, number of levels, and assessment style among groups, making it difficult to carry generalization too far. Harding, Page and Rowell (1980) regard the involvement of teachers in defining syllabuses and producing tests as invaluable, and point out that teachers 'can use their joint experience to produce tests which are more polished than tests produced by one or two teachers in a single school' (p. 36). Not all teachers are familiar with the theoretical background to the GOML approach, and Harding, Page and Rowell stress the in-service value to teachers in participating in the activities of the groups. As far as the pupils are concerned, 'The tests set out to show what learners can do, rather than what they cannot. Competition between learners is also excluded: the only competitive element is between the individual learner's motivation and the task to be accomplished' (p. 33).

Pupil motivation is a major concern of two evaluation studies, by Buckby *et al.* (1981) of schemes in Leeds and North Yorkshire and by Freedman (1982) of the East Midlands scheme. Both these studies report positive motivational effects, for example:

> The pupils' responses to their five attitude questions showed that the majority were enjoying both the teaching and the assessment aspects of the work, and these findings are substantiated by their voluntary comments. These comments also reveal considerable enthusiasm and positive motivation (Freedman, 1982, p. 72).

However, these evaluations were carried out early in the development of the schemes, and further evaluation would be desirable.

The East Midlands scheme is interesting in several ways. It is an early example of cooperation between an examination board, a university school of education, local education authorities and teachers in schools to develop a graded assessment scheme (Dunning, 1983). The term assessment is used since in this case there are no centrally devised tests. 'Instead, the assessment syllabus guidelines set out the language functions to be mastered, and describe the assessment *procedures* to which the teachers are required to conform' (Freedman, 1982, p. 25). This leads to particular stress on in-service education for teachers, and on methods for standardization of assessments.

Three schemes (Oxfordshire, Leeds and Lancs/Cumbria) are the subject of reports by HMI (1983; 1985 a; 1985 b). The principal method of data collection is classroom observation, and these reports focus on the impact of the schemes on the teaching and learning of languages. While praising positive effects such as increased pupil enthusiasm, HMI found classroom practice to be variable in quality, and they express certain reservations including criticisms of excessive use of English, of the use of test syllabuses as teaching syllabuses and of the entry of some pupils for tests before they are ready. HMI argue for continued emphasis on in-service training and in one report conclude that 'Greater attention now needs to be given to pace, progression and methodology so that one of the primary aims of the proponents of graded tests, an improvement in the foreign language acquisition and performance of young people, may be effectively achieved' (HMI, 1985 b, p. 11).

A specific concern about the GOML approach referred to by Page (1983) is that it

> may lead to the learning and parroting of a few phrases to be used as tokens in a narrow range of situations and the fossilisation of a sort of pidgin leading to a failure to acquire a generative capacity that can cope with new situations and the need for new meanings (Page, 1983, p. 303).

Harrison (1982) points out that there are practical constraints on teachers who introduce GOML schemes, and it appears that a pragmatic approach is often adopted. 'Many issues have been difficult to resolve, and rather than hold up the progress of a scheme from design stage to realization in practice, some groups have put off central problems for later discussion' (Harrison, 1982, p. 49).

In this book we focus on the GOML scheme developed in West Sussex, and report data from case studies of three schools. Schools P and Q are mixed 11–18 comprehensives, the former serving a rural catchment area and the latter situated in a housing estate in a seaside town. School R is a 13–18 comprehensive, and takes boys and girls from a wide range of backgrounds.

The West Sussex GOALS Scheme

Work on GOALS (Graded Objectives for Achievement in Language Skills) began in 1978, and a level 1 French syllabus and tests became available to all secondary schools in West Sussex in September 1979 as the result of development by working parties of teachers within the county, along guidelines formulated by a Steering Committee chaired by the Modern Languages Adviser. Harding, Page and Rowell (1980) in a description of the GOALS scheme, point out that it is based on notional/functional syllabus design, and has been influenced by the Council of Europe 'Threshold level' investigations and by the thinking of John Clark's Lothian group. The scheme has developed rapidly, with support from the West Sussex LEA, and in 1985 there were five levels in French and two in German, with levels 3 and 4 German in preparation; levels 1 and 2 Spanish were also under development. In French, level 4 was available as a Mode 3 CSE through the Southern Regional Examination Board (SREB), and level 5 was examined for the first time in summer 1985 as a Mode 3 O-level through the Associated Examining Board (AEB).

The group has made no attempt to design a course as such. However the syllabuses are detailed and there is a 'teacher's pack' available for each level. In addition to the syllabus and tests themselves, this includes notes for teachers on appropriate teaching methods and materials, instructions for administering the tests, oral practice cards, pupil checklists and record sheets. Productive and receptive linguistic items are distinguished in the syllabuses, which are not restricted to lists of functions and notions, but also include interpersonal topics, survival topics and background information. Syllabuses in German follow the pattern established in French. At levels 1 and 2 there are reading, listening and speaking tests, the latter being subdivided into oral assignments, role-play and structured conversation. Successful candidates must pass in each macro-skill, the pass marks at level 1 being 24/40 for the speaking and listening tests, 10/20 for the reading/background test.* An optional writing test is introduced at level 3, where a pass becomes based on an aggregate score; at levels 4 and 5 there are compulsory tests in all four macro-skills, which of course satisfy the Mode 3 requirements of the respective examining boards. GOALS certificates at each level are issued to successful candidates by the West Sussex County Council.

Which pupils take which levels is a matter of school policy. At school P the head of department sees no particular virtue in forcing everyone to go through every level. This is time-consuming, and for some pupils a bit too easy, as well as increasing teacher workloads. Many pupils, therefore, will bypass one or more levels, and it is certainly not felt at this school that mastery at one level must be demonstrated before moving to the next. Staff have considerable freedom in deciding whether to enter pupils for particular

---

*These details were correct at the time of the fieldwork. Levels 1 and 2 in French have since been revised in the light of six years' experience with the scheme.

levels, and to some extent when to enter them. Factors taken into account include pupil motivation; pupil readiness; whether practice in test technique is needed; whether time is available to administer the oral tests; and teacher workload.

GOALS Assessment

Readiness

The scheme allows tests to be taken at any time during the year, and it is a principle of the graded test movement that tests should be taken only when pupils are ready, in order to encourage success. A GOALS document (West Sussex, 1981) makes this clear: 'To enter groups of learners for the tests before virtually all are both confident and capable of success would be to do them a disservice.' All GOALS tests except the orals are intended to be administered during normal foreign language lessons to class groups rather than to individuals. The teacher must select a date when the syllabus has been covered and the class as a whole is felt to be ready. In practice courses are often arranged so that the ground for a particular level is covered by the end of the school year, so that GOALS reading and listening tests (and the level 3 writing test) can be taken as end-of-year examinations. Since pupils do not all progress at the same rate, even where there is setting, and groups do not necessarily take one year to cover one level, some pupils are entered for GOALS tests before they are ready. Other pupils may be ready early, but have to wait until the end of the year to be tested.

> Ideally they should be able to go in for whatever level when they're ready, and if you could work it in practical terms, it would be fine ... We just can't do it; it is impossible to administer it. If we could do, it would be all the motivation that we need, because there is a progression there which is very useful (teacher).

Other teachers argued that it would only be possible to permit flexibility in individual entry so as to test pupils when they are genuinely ready if cover were to be provided so that one teacher could supervise the class while another conducted the testing; this would require an increase in staffing.

The 'structured conversation' and 'role-play' components of the oral test require the whole syllabus to have been covered, and are likely to be taken at the same time as the reading and listening tests, although oral testing is done on an individual basis. It is also possible for the 'oral assignments' to be left to the end of the year, but in most cases these are spread through the year (there are five sections). Here there is the possibility that pupils could be tested when they are individually ready, that is, a pupil could ask to be tested when he or she had prepared for a particular section, and this is suggested on the oral assessment sheets. Some staff do allow pupils to decide for themselves when they are ready for oral assignment tests.

> I go through all the vocabulary they need for each section. We practise it together round the class. They practise it in pairs. As soon as they're ready to be tested, they come and be tested. Well the slower ones take longer to learn and practise and you find somebody's on Section 4 and somebody's still on Section 1 (teacher).

Eventually it is necessary to chase up some pupils, and to tell them when they are to be tested. One teacher had tried letting pupils (in a low set) decide, but had abandoned this: 'the assignments were taking ages and ages . . . You know, it says tell your teacher when you're ready. Well, they were never ready. Always an excuse why they couldn't do it.'

A second reason for not allowing pupils to decide when they are tested is that oral assignment testing occupies considerable time, and it is much simpler to test the whole class on a section, one at a time, but on days specified in advance by the teacher.

> They have to be ready for them when I'm ready for them . . . I will teach the points as best I can, and make sure as far as I can that as many people in the class are as au fait with the situation as possible, and then I'll get down to testing it. I'm frankly not going to be messing about testing a little bit for this kid in September and the same item for somebody else in November. I can't keep myself straight in those circumstances. I wouldn't know where I was, and I would prefer to know that we have got through this or that particular aspect more or less at one time (teacher).

In summary, staff find it hard to apply the principle of readiness because of practical considerations and constraints.

Oral testing: an example

In an observed period, a 1st-year class was being tested on level 1 oral assignments. The first ten minutes were spent with the children practising in pairs, using sets of cards produced by the GOALS scheme. Each card had a question on one side, for example *Say that your name is Mary*, and the answer *Je m'appelle Marie* on the other; several different sets were available. The teacher walked round the class, giving assistance and encouragement. Most children seemed to be working effectively, and to be enjoying it. The noise level was moderate, and there was little apparent time-wasting, although the opportunity was there. In the next five minutes, some pairs were asked to perform for the class. Most could answer confidently and correctly, although some were hard to hear.

The actual testing then started, with pupils coming up one at a time to be tested by the teacher. They were keen to come up, and there was no problem with others hearing the testing since there was sufficient space between the teacher's dais and the class. Tests took about three minutes each. After three tests, the teacher stopped the class; she was not satisfied with the standard: 'You don't come out for a test until you know all ten perfectly and off by heart.' Pupils not being tested were practising, using the check-list produced by the scheme, stuck in their exercise books. This contains five blocks of ten items. Some pupils were practising seriously, but others were just chatting, and it was necessary for the teacher to stop testing from time to time, to maintain control of the class. Pupils who had been tested could prepare for the next section or be set extra work from the textbook.

Pupils were clearly pleased and relieved when they passed a section; other pupils sometimes asked them whether they had passed when they returned to their seats. Some who were questioned by the researcher said they liked the tests, and thought it made them learn the material; the level of difficulty seemed to be about right. They didn't mind waiting to be tested, and thought it was quite an easy period! It is not an easy period for the teacher, who said one had to be feeling A1 to do GOALS testing; she would only spend one lesson per week completely on GOALS testing with any one class.

Oral testing: discussion

There is a danger of teachers being swamped by the sheer volume of testing. At school Q several teachers said they had left testing until too late the previous year, and had then been faced with considerable pressure towards the end of year; in some cases it had proved impossible to complete testing, and in others it had only been completed by devices such as extracting pupils from other lessons during free periods, or devoting all periods to testing and setting pupils to do time-filling tasks while others were tested; some testing had been carried out at lunchtimes. It was pointed out that if GOALS was extended to more classes, the strain on teachers might become intolerable.

Most testing was carried out during normal language periods, in or just outside the room. For example:

it was just a case of moving a few desks, and I could sit with my back to the wall . . . facing the backs of the class, so that I could see what was going on. They would have some work to do, or they would be working in pairs testing themselves, and I could get through about 10 or 12 during the course of a 55-minute period (teacher).

Whether individual tests average three or five minutes does of course affect very considerably the total time devoted to testing.

Several staff mentioned the difficulties of setting work to occupy the rest of the class while testing is in progress, in what is fundamentally an oral/aural course. 'I've usually got some form of worksheet or something from the textbook that the rest just get on with . . . Some of them get on with it, some of them don't!' (teacher). There is therefore a danger that pupils will become bored, waste time, or become noisy while oral testing is in progress. In another observed period, with a pleasant and well-disciplined 4th-year class, it was necessary for the teacher to stop testing several times in order to reduce the noise from the class to an acceptable level (i.e. to be fair to those being tested).

Of the teachers who had tried doing some of the testing during lunchtimes, one had found after a time that the pupils were reluctant to come, and another felt that it was not satisfactory, since both pupils and teachers needed a break. Again, it was felt that the only satisfactory solution would be to arrange cover, so that one teacher could concentrate on the testing while another looked after the class. There is not only the question of discipline, but also the problem that pupils are receiving no actual teaching while testing is taking place. At school Q it had been possible to arrange cover when main school teachers had been free as a result of classes taking public examinations, but it was not realistic to carry out all GOALS testing during this period. Another suggestion was to use the language assistants to help with testing. At least one member of staff feels that this issue of the organization of oral testing is the critical one for GOALS, and that the success of the scheme as a whole depends on its being resolved in a satisfactory way. Not only is oral testing dependent on the cooperation of the class, which may not always be forthcoming, but also 'it is extremely time-consuming. If there were a means of cutting down the amount of time that we had to spend in order for the assessments to be made, then I would be in favour of that (teacher)'. The organization of oral testing remains a problem, although it is regarded as an essential part of the GOALS scheme.* No difficulties were reported in organizing other components of the tests (reading, listening, writing).

*The volume of oral testing in French levels 1 and 2 has in fact now been reduced.

Some technical issues

General satisfaction was expressed by staff on the quality and validity of the GOALS tests. However some teachers argued that, although the testing is a valid exercise if the course has been taught appropriately, it is possible to get through GOALS by 'parroting', that is, without genuine learning. Indeed one teacher felt that it is difficult to teach pupils to do some of the assignments *without* parroting.

> The listening and the reading tests are fine, and I think the role plays are good. The assignments, some of them are good, some of them aren't. How do you teach them that you've got to say "I don't like it"? They've got to be able to say that one sentence.

In an observed session the test was on hotel situations, for example, 'Ask for a double room with a shower.' The pupils had the French phrases written out in their exercise books, and were tested on a proportion of them. At the end, the teacher told the class that some had rehearsed their answers, and did not sound natural. This may be an inevitable difficulty with a testing scheme which clearly specifies the tasks to be performed by candidates.

The rules for administering and marking the tests are felt to be clear.

> Marking schemes, I would have thought they are totally reliable because it's multiple choice; both the reading and listening comprehensions . . . are totally objective. The speaking, I suppose there is an element of subjectivity comes into that . . . At the same time, it's not too difficult because we lay down for each speaking utterance either a 0,1 scale or a 0,1,2 scale, and there's quite a lot in print about when to give 1 out of 2 (head of dept.).

Some felt that there was perhaps too much in print: 'It's not very complicated, actually. It's just that before you do any one test you've got to read maybe 3 sides of A4' (teacher).

Staff were satisfied that the tests are fair, and that they are administered in such a way that pupils are unable to cheat. They were confident that results are independent of the particular teacher, and that other schools would mark in the same way. The GOALS scheme has opted for producing detailed marking schemes, and there is no moderation system for levels 1–3.

The marks required to obtain a pass on each component are regarded as about right. 'They certainly shouldn't be lower. I think that they are low enough for the majority of children to reach that standard, but high enough for them to have attained a satisfactory level. I wouldn't necessarily say a good level' (teacher).

At level 1 most pupils score far more than the required marks and teachers expect them to do so, but it is accepted that the standard should be within reach of almost all children and that level 2 demands a significantly higher standard. Perfection is not necessary for survival communication, and the criterion 'understandable by a sympathetic native speaker' is thought to be fair and realistic. One teacher was doubtful about level 3; he felt that pupils should demonstrate an improvement in pronunciation, intonation and fluency at higher levels, and that more rigid guidelines were needed as to what is acceptable and what is not.

The certificates list the skills acquired and state the marks required to pass. There were mixed feelings on the question of whether pupils succeeding at a particular level have actually acquired the skills listed on the back of the certificates. GOALS is felt to be an advance on traditional tests in terms of precision and relevance, but several teachers argued that some pupils would 'mug up' the materials for the test, and not retain the knowledge or skills, although this applies to almost any test. One teacher criticized the language used on the certificates as being too adult for the child to relate the stated skills to what he could do. Another teacher argued that if the certificates were to have value in the outside world, it would be necessary to inform employers and others of the meaning of the certificates, and convince them of their validity.

One further issue is the relationship of GOALS to overall school policy on assessment. In school P's internal assessment system for reporting to parents, assessment is relative to the rest of the set, not to the whole year-group; no rank order is produced, but there are five-point scales for effort and for achievement, allocated by the set teacher. There appears to be no conflict with GOALS assessment, and indeed GOALS tests are often taken as part of internal school examinations.

At school Q although surprisingly few problems have arisen, end-of-year reports still contain examination percentages and positions. This is against the spirit of GOALS, which is not designed to discriminate between candidates, and one teacher expressed the view that the assessment system should either be all GOALS or not GOALS at all.

Mastery learning and re-takes

There is no consistent pattern within or between case-study schools on which pupils are entered for which GOALS levels, and which levels are bypassed. However in most cases entry for GOALS tests is by whole classes, with the consequence that some pupils are likely not to be ready and to fail. With weak sets this could be between one-third and one-half of the set. There is then the question of what to do with those individuals, who will not be sufficiently numerous to form a complete set. 'If you've failed level 1, and you've actually worked at all for it, you're not going to get level 2. I think that's fairly evident' (teacher). However it is possible to continue with level 2 work with the class, since level 2 subsumes level 1, and when it comes to take the tests either to allow the level 1 failures to take the level 2 tests irrespective of their failure, or to arrange for those pupils to re-take the level 1 tests (or equivalently at higher levels).

In practice, school P has had few pupils re-taking tests since it is difficult to organize and since few have asked to re-sit. This is partly because the school takes the view that those who fail must re-take all components of the test, even those on which a pass has been obtained. However this seems to be a misinterpretation of the rules of the scheme, which state that 'individual tests may be re-taken in case of "failure", after a suitable period of consolidation' (West Sussex, 1981). It is *not* permissible to re-take individual oral assignments, but it is possible to re-take the whole of them, while carrying forward passes obtained on other test components. Several staff expressed their concern that pupils who did badly on early oral assignments might realize that they were going to fail, and give up. Although failure and the possibility of re-taking tests only affects a minority of pupils overall, it does seem to be an area requiring further consideration. The scheme does not produce new tests at levels 1–3 each year, so it is necessary for pupils to re-sit the same tests, but this is not seen as a problem.

Mastery learning depends on the opportunity to retake tests in the event of failure, and the Head of Department R said that they do try to offer this opportunity to pupils who have failed on one section (for example the reading or listening test), but that in practice pressure of work has made it not always possible, and that it depends on pupils asking to be retested. Another member of the department said that ideally they would like pupils to pass each level in turn.

> It would be quite difficult, I think, to come into graded tests at a
> higher level without having done it lower down. I think the pupils
> would get confused, and I think the teachers would find it difficult
> to know what they were aiming at (teacher).

Since pupils who fail a level cannot always re-take, and since some levels are bypassed, GOALS is not operated as a mastery learning programme in the sense that pupils take the tests for the levels in strict progression, and do not study for level n+1 until they have demonstrated mastery at level n. It is difficult to apply these principles unless learning is individualized. But it was pointed out that bypassing the actual tests does not mean that mastery of that level has not been attained; the ground will still be covered and assessed internally. However the concepts of mastery learning do not seem to be prominent in the minds of staff, although the sequence of GOALS levels is such that each depends on what has gone before. Several teachers at school Q argued that it is not possible to have different members of a class preparing for different levels at the same time. 'To be oscillating between various assignments for level 1 and level 2 within any one period, I feel that you would end up by wasting an awful lot of time in the sheer complexities of what's involved' (teacher). So those pupils in 2nd-year classes who had failed GOALS 1 are preparing for GOALS 2; in fact the syllabus for level 2 is largely refinement and extension of level 1, involving the same topics. One teacher had abandoned an attempt to get level 1 failures to re-take the tests. As another teacher pointed out: 'We're going to have to face the situation, regardless of the possibility of people repeating things . . . that in fact people are going to fail. Then we've got to ask ourselves what are we going to do.'

The problem really arises at level 2 in French; in one example quoted to the researcher a 3rd-year set which had not done GOALS 1 was entered for GOALS 2, and 19 out of 31 passed. Presumably the others were not ready. One teacher thought that if GOALS is extended into the 4th and 5th years, there might be pupils at three different levels in the same group, and that some way must be found of preventing this; one possibility is to introduce mixed-age grouping. 'For the sake of the unity of the class and the sanity of the teacher', as another teacher put it, it is best to have the whole group working at the same thing. This teacher stressed the difficulty of inheriting a class with mixed GOALS history.

Public examinations

Traditional O-level and CSE examinations were criticized for including obscure vocabulary and situations. The GOALS mode 3 examinations were developed in order that 4th- and 5th-year pupils may both continue with a GOALS-based course and have the opportunity to obtain CSE or GCE certification. Schools P and R have entered candidates for these examinations. Several staff have attended consortium meetings (for standardization and moderation) for the existing level 4 (CSE) and the new level 5 (O-level). There was no doubt at school P that these exams are of an equivalent standard to traditional examinations. Nor were serious doubts expressed about the major difference that these exams have with graded tests, namely a range of grades rather than a simple pass/fail; the Head of Department P argued for public examination results to be expressed as a profile of performance in the four macro-skills as well as a single grade. He felt that with the advent of a new GCSE examination along GOALS lines, levels 4 and 5 might not be needed any more. The department is confident that this new exam will be in line with their approach to teaching languages.

At school R, the two upper 5th-year sets have been entered for the new GOALS level 5 mode 3 O-level examination in French, and the two members of the department who have taught these sets have conducted the oral testing, as well as attending panel meetings for preparation of the examination and for standardization. The Head of Department is marking the reading scripts for all candidates entered from schools in the consortium. Looking towards GCSE, she said: 'We are aware that the work which has been invested this year is in fact going to make life easier for us in years to come.'

One teacher reported some pupil doubts about whether it is a real O-level (although it is certificated by the AEB in just the same way as any other O-level). Another is pleased that it seems to tie in much more with what she called a 'CSE mentality', in that it is more teacher-based, and that teachers can discuss standards in panel meetings. Other staff also welcome the move towards teacher assessment, but are not satisfied with the payments being made for their work, and feel that the level of in-service training provided by the examination board needs to be improved, specifically in the area of oral examining. While attendance at meetings is a valuable form of in-service, it is not enough. They have found the marking scheme too complex for marking to take place during the oral examination.

In the case of the Mode 3 CSE (GOALS level 4) there appear to have been few problems. Marking is internal, but all tapes of oral tests (except oral assignments) and all scripts for the writing paper are sent to the external moderator.

Suitability Across the Ability Range

Mixed-ability groups at school Q

When department Q introduced mixed-ability teaching into the 1st year several staff had been opposed to the decision. However, it was so successful that it was proposed, and accepted by a large majority, to extend it into the 2nd year the following year, maintaining the same groups and where possible the same teachers.

It was generally felt that the GOALS level 1 tests are suitable for the whole ability range. Reasons put forward for teaching mixed-ability groups included the difficulty of differentiating between pupils other than the very weak and the very able, and the desirability of having 'leaders' in a class to assist the progress of the class as a whole. The Head of Department feels that the loss of these leaders as a result of a setting process has a disorienting effect on a class. However some staff were finding difficulty in teaching mixed-ability 2nd-year classes. One problem is in dealing with those (few) pupils who have failed GOALS 1. Another is that GOALS 2 is felt to be considerably more difficult than GOALS 1 for the less able children, the better children being at an advantage because of greater capacity for recall, greater fluency and better response to the testing situation. Other teachers were happier about the suitability of GOALS 2 for less able pupils, but did not think whole classes could be ready for tests by the end of the 2nd year. It had in fact been suggested that GOALS 2 could be used as a criterion for entry into 3rd-year top sets; no one felt that mixed-ability teaching would be viable in the 3rd year. It was realized that it would not be satisfactory to enter whole classes for GOALS 2 tests and have a high failure rate, both from the point of view of morale, and because of the difficulty of dealing with groups some who have and some who have not passed level 2. In any case GOALS 2 may be an appropriate objective for many pupils by the end of Year 3. Extra material is available in the text-book for faster pupils, and teachers would expect a higher standard of accuracy from them in GOALS work, and for them to be more ambitious in role-play exercises. The Head of Department argued that there are plenty of ways in which these pupils can exploit their French without just moving on faster, although he accepted that there is a danger that some may become bored in a mixed-ability group. He feels that it is possible to teach towards GOALS in such a way that virtually everyone can attain mastery, although some might find recall very difficult.

Suitability for less able pupils

At school R, GOALS level 1 in German has been found to be suitable right across the ability range in mixed-ability 3rd-year classes. In the case of 3rd-year French, where almost all pupils have studied the language for three years before they arrive at the school, broad setting and careful choice of course enable the staff to cope with a wide range of ability, and GOALS is felt to be suitable for all pupils: 'I'm quite happy with what it's doing across the ability range' (head of 3rd year). However, pass rates for GOALS level 2 in 3rd-year lower sets suggest that, although the course may be suitable, the level 2 tests are too hard for many pupils, or they cannot reach the necessary standard by the end of the year. In 1984, of the three sets, one group was not entered since their teacher thought they were not ready. The other two sets were entered, but only 38 per cent passed. The head of department was surprised and disappointed by this figure. In her view, 'We must make sure that at the end of the 3rd year ... every student finishes with a feeling of success with regard to their French.'

There were also difficulties for lower 4th-year sets taking GOALS level 3, where the pass rate for two sets in 1984 was 41 per cent, although pupils in the two upper sets all passed. The school is discontinuing entry for level 3, mainly for logistic reasons, but level 3 would appear not to be suitable for many pupils in the lower half of those who have opted for French in the 4th year. Nevertheless these same pupils almost all achieve a grading in level 4 (CSE Mode 3) at the end of the 5th year.

At both other case-study schools there were doubts about GOALS for the weakest pupils, particularly after level 1, since the scheme requires a retentive memory and reasonable reading ability, even though it is predominantly an oral/aural course, since pupils need to read, for example, their own notes.

> I wish I could feel really convinced that I was achieving very much more with less able youngsters. I'm not sure that it is a fact that the less able youngster can learn to speak the language better than he ever could learn it on a more grammatical-type approach. I'm not convinced that he gets very much further (teacher).

However, other teachers expressed stronger support for GOALS: 'It's infinitely better than doing anything else. They can cope with it, remotely, and some of them even come to cope with it fairly competently' (teacher).

Suitability for potential A-level candidates

Some staff felt that GOALS level 1 tests are much too easy for the most able pupils, but it is of course possible to bypass these. In both French and German, GOALS is supplemented for able pupils, principally by extra written work.

A concern was that it might be difficult for sixth formers to make the jump from a GOALS course to a traditional A-level with a strong literature component. One head of department argued that existing A-level courses produce 'virtually useless skills', and is strongly in favour of examination reform. But other interviewees felt that, given that the scheme is supplemented with grammar, GOALS is at least as suitable as previous courses for leading on to A-level.

Staff Opinion on the Impact of GOALS

Impact on teaching and learning

The introduction of GOALS has had significant effects on curriculum and pedagogy. A teacher at school Q said, 'it's had a fair amount of impact inasmuch as all sections of the department now are forced to look at a much more oral approach to the teaching than perhaps was in evidence before the appearance of GOALS'. Several members of the department had already moved in that direction, but GOALS has accelerated the change in teaching style. However GOALS requires much more than an emphasis on oral work. An observed lesson with a 5th-year German group who are working on a traditional syllabus was almost entirely oral, but could probably not have been a GOALS lesson for several reasons. Firstly it was based on a picture story rather than a communicative situation; secondly there was no interaction between pupils; and thirdly the accent was on structure and on accuracy.

GOALS is seen as requiring a very substantial change in modern-language teaching: 'Really the whole emphasis of language has changed to a means of communication, the spoken word, which frankly is what language is all about' (teacher). The shift is away from translation towards practical use of the language in real situations; the survival aspect was praised by several staff. One stressed the importance of making the work appear real to individual pupils, but mentioned the need for care, for example in dealing with the family situation for pupils from non-standard families. Another felt that it became more difficult to make the work authentic and avoid artificiality once pupils got beyond level 1.

Since the schools are in a relatively prosperous area of the country adjacent to the Channel, it is likely that many pupils will actually use their languages abroad, on school trips or family holidays. Commercially produced tapes using native speakers at normal conversational speed were used in several of the observed lessons for listening comprehension, and staff at school P emphasized the importance of listening as well as speaking. 'It gets them to speak French, which in the past has been laughed at . . . And the listening, which was practically ignored before; listening I find is *the* most important. Now if you can get the gist of what somebody's saying' (teacher). The point that exact translation and grammatical accuracy are no longer necessary was made by several staff. What matters in GOALS is to understand, and communicate, in real situations.

> Head of department: . . . we think, or we flatter ourselves, that we've got, even as tests, things that could happen in real life. All right, we make a bit of make-believe about it, but everyone knows that they might

arrive in a hotel in France some time, and they might not be able to speak any English there, and therefore you've got to cope. So that is a test, but it's also an occurrence, a situation, that they could meet up with.

Researcher: And they perceive it as real, do they, or do they think it's make-believe?

Head of department: Well we tell them that it's make-believe as well, because it's in the classroom, but I think it's reasonably easy to persuade them that this could happen to them. I've never actually had anybody say to me 'Well this is all rubbish because I shall never go to France.' They haven't reacted in that way . . .

He regards it as important that pupils should be able to say the right thing in real life, not that they should be able to write phrases, or have a neat exercise book. Pupils have to be given time to prepare to say things, and progress often appears to be slow, with the teacher resisting the temptation to press on.

In the old days at the end of the lesson you could usually look through an exercise book and see how much a child had written, and how much they'd got right . . . With the new way you either can't assess at all how much you've got through, or it seems to be far less, but I don't know whether in fact it is (head of dept.).

He sees the GOALS approach as a major revolution in what teachers do and how they do it.

At school Q it was generally agreed that pupil competence and confidence at speaking the language had increased significantly as a result of the introduction of GOALS:

I'm sure that the reluctance of the past, people not wishing to open their mouths, or not being able to open their mouths and let anything coherent come out, has gone. Lots of these kids are now prepared to have a go, and I think that is a move in the right direction (teacher).

Another teacher was certain that GOALS helps to overcome the psychological barrier of speaking the foreign language, and that pupils would be more likely to be able to cope later on, for example on the telephone. One interesting difficulty is in convincing pupils that talking, as opposed to writing, is a valid form of work.

A lot of them do tend to come and say 'We haven't done anything this last 3 weeks, sir. Look, nothing in our books!' That's their

> attitude. I say 'Hang on, it's a spoken language, and we're trying to get you to speak the language, and if you've made progress and you can say 10 more things this week than you could last week, then you're working.' But it is difficult (teacher).

As pointed out above, the lack of writing makes it more difficult also for teachers to monitor pupil progress, or to judge how well the course is going. The GOALS tests themselves may fulfil a useful role in that respect. Several staff mentioned the importance of retaining some writing in the course, but there were no doubts about the move towards spoken French and German.

> I'm absolutely certain that we're going in the right direction, inasmuch as the language should of course first of all be spoken. Most of the children that we deal with have little recourse to written French. They might need to read it, but more than anything else they'll be likely to speak it (teacher).

Aspects of the testing structure

The change to a communicative approach appears to be the main reason for staff to favour GOALS, but there was also support for the testing structure: 'I think from the point of view of graded tests we're going in the right way. It gives them a limited objective which they know they can achieve, so that's a good thing' (teacher).

Monitoring student progress is clearly felt to be important in a communicative approach to the language, and the oral assignment testing can help in this, although one teacher warned of the risk of overemphasis on testing, which she felt could take pace out of the teaching, particularly with the more able pupils. The fact that GOALS is task-orientated, with precise statements of what pupils have to aim for and achieve was welcomed by staff.

> I think that's a great advantage of them, that you have got rigid standards to go by ... It works sufficiently well for you to be able to swap over teachers half way through a year and still carry on, with no problems ... If everyone's doing the same thing towards the same end, then it does make life a lot easier (teacher).

This consistency of approach was also felt to be helpful where shared sets are necessary.

However the fact that GOALS is a testing rather than a teaching syllabus means that staff must adapt textbook material, being selective and adding in extra bits where necessary, particularly in the periods leading up to GOALS tests, to ensure that pupils have covered the specified vocabulary and tasks.

Staff at all three schools were concerned at the volume and complexity of the work which they need to undertake in order to integrate GOALS syllabuses and textbook materials into a coherent course suitable for the particular class being taught. Teachers found difficulty in selecting and combining materials from different sources, and it was suggested by one that GOALS should be developed into an integrated course.

Another common concern at the case study schools is the danger of parroting, which is strongly discouraged by a scheme document.

> Any attempt to present syllabus items as forms to be simply 'learnt by heart' and then tested would be a reversion to the worst traditions of phrase book memorisation and recall, without active involvement or understanding, and would represent a travesty of the intentions of those who devised the scheme (West Sussex, 1981).

Staff are aware that it is possible to teach for GOALS in a way that is not genuinely communicative and that pupils might pass tests purely by relying on memory; it is difficult for staff to discourage this since they wish to encourage success.

> I'm guilty of occasionally writing on the board 'This is what you must learn, and learn it', which is really bad. I know it's really bad, but for some of them I don't know how else to do it. Perhaps it'll come with practice. (teacher).

It was recognized that particularly towards the end of the school year, when teachers are under pressure and are anxious to get GOALS testing completed, there is a tendency to turn to the checklist and drill particular items until they are known. This suggests that success in GOALS tests may not necessarily denote mastery of the material in terms of real understanding or retention of knowledge. However, staff also felt that GOALS could be taught in such a way as to avoid parroting. Ideally, the GOALS items would occur, and recur, naturally in the course of teaching the language.

A related issue is future build-up of the ability to manipulate language by pupils following GOALS-based courses: 'Whether by doing too much parrot-fashion stuff up to level 4 . . . they will still be as good at creating their own French sentences, I'm not sure' (teacher). There is a possibility that, because the tasks to be performed are clearly specified at each level, pupils will never reach a 'take-off' point at which they can produce things that they haven't been taught.

The Head of Department P feels that there are similar problems with conventional syllabuses, and that if pupils understand functions they can apply them to different parallel situations. He argued that in teaching for GOALS more time is spent in going over different ways in which things can be expressed, and gave the example of 'you must', 'it is necessary' and 'you've got to' all being expressed in French by 'il faut'. Certainly if his school's curriculum aim of moving away from a knowledge emphasis towards a problem-solving, creative and skills base is to be attained in the case of GOALS, pupils must understand what they have learnt sufficiently well to apply their vocabulary and knowledge of functions to unfamiliar situations, not just those specified in the syllabus and hence memorizable.

One teacher was concerned that GOALS is insufficiently analytical:

> They've been saying 'je voudrais' for a whole year, and they don't know what 'would like' is; they don't even know what 'I' is! So we're not teaching them language really. We're teaching them certain communicative powers, but we're not teaching them about language and how it works any more; we're just teaching them how to get certain messages across.

She felt that it was important not only to teach pupils how to do something, but also how to use their minds, that is, how to work out how to do something. Traditional courses enabled pupils to reach the take-off point at which they could use the written language creatively; she hoped that GOALS could encourage the creative use of spoken language, and thought that pupils should be shown examples of such use.

Pupil motivation: certificates, success

At school P most staff comment on pupil motivation related to 2nd-, 3rd- and 4th-year pupils, who are not preparing for public examinations at the end of the year. One teacher felt that GOALS had little effect.

> I think if the pupils are going to *be* motivated, they will be anyway. I haven't found that the GOALS testing has made them any more motivated or less motivated . . . They're keen to get the certificates when they've got that far, but when they start I find that they're not particularly interested with the certificates.

Another, referring to a low 4th-year set, thought that for some of the set, 'they'll follow the course, but they won't be that motivated by the idea of getting a GOALS certificate'. Other teachers thought that the certificates themselves did act as a motivator: 'The lower ability ones, obviously it's great for them to get a certificate . . . They're actually good at something. They've got something to prove it.' This teacher had found, however, that some pupils didn't like to be presented with their certificates in assembly, since they felt embarrassed. Another had no hesitation in using the certificates as a carrot for a 2nd-year set.

> You can't start explaining to them the philosophy behind GOALS, so you've got to promise them something . . . and even though it's been going on in the school for a few years now, I've never seen anybody rip a GOALS certificate up, or not be proud of it.

There were also rather mixed feelings at school Q about the value of the certificates themselves. Some staff think that they are quite an important incentive, in providing tangible proof of attainment, but it was pointed out that for some younger children it is too long-term, even though the scheme aims to provide short-term goals. One teacher felt that the certificates do not make much difference to motivation: 'I've given out certificates, and people have been pleased initially, and the next week you find the certificates still stuffed in the bottom of their bags or creased up.'

Parental attitudes were mentioned as a factor, and it was thought that most parents know little about GOALS; although an information sheet is available, this is written for the pupils, who may or may not take it home. 'One of the problems is that parents don't value it [the certificate] . . . particularly with the less able, less motivated children' (teacher). This teacher had arranged for the head of year to present the certificates; the headmaster had not been asked to present GOALS certificates, but would be willing to do so. No global records had been kept in the school for the number of certificates presented, but the head of department feels that certificates are an important part of motivation. The function of certificates is seen as motivational rather than as providing an accurate description of what pupils can do.

It was felt by several staff at school P that GOALS could have negative as well as positive motivational effects – or that it could be neutral.

> It's a double-edged sword, isn't it, because the good children don't need motivation. They have it anyway, and they're really pleased to get the certificate . . . The bad kids, they do need the motivation, and they do get that motivation, but at the same time they also get the reinforcement of failure because a lot of them do fail and they know that they've failed. So it's got both. It will motivate them, but it'll also make them more aware of their inadequacies.

The main difficulty is with those who fail to reach level 1, since they often realize they are going to fail at an early stage, even though teachers avoid telling them this: 'They knew they'd failed the reading test, but I didn't actually say to them "You've failed the whole thing because of this", because it's so demoralising.'

One or two teachers felt that pupils get fed up with the actual testing, which is undoubtedly time-consuming, but the head of department expressed a different view.

> There's not so much mystery about these tests any more, so that I think some children quite like the tests themselves, provided you've told them quite honestly what it'll be like . . . I think possibly they now feel that we're not always trying to catch them out in exams.

Another teacher saw the main virtue of the tests as being a provider of short-term attainment goals.

At school Q, GOALS level 1 French was generally thought to have a positive motivating effect, because it is appropriate, practical and useful, and because it enables a high proportion of children to achieve, and experience, success. A teacher expressed the view that the tests should be taken without pressure. However, there were doubts about GOALS French level 2, where the success rate is much lower; large numbers of failures cannot be beneficial.

Pupil motivation: competition

The issue of competition between pupils arose particularly at school Q.

> It's a very strange attitude here. Open antipathy. Anyone who does well is a 'boff', and is singled out for ridicule and mocking. And it tends to make people, even the bright ones, not want to show that they're doing too much work, or doing too well. It's very sad (teacher).

This attitude may perhaps best be tackled by a system of assessment which is non-competitive, and GOALS may be seen in this light. 'A lot of competition used to stem from marks, and I find myself giving fewer and fewer tests and marked pieces of work, inevitably' (teacher). The same teacher developed an aspect of graded test philosophy:

> I think that there is considerably less competition than there was. I don't think that people compete with each other in the same way at all. I think it's a bit more healthy in a way, inasmuch as I suppose the better ones, or the more motivated ones, compete with themselves, inasmuch as they like to achieve success in the particular part of the test that you're aiming at, and eventually gain a certificate.

The head of department does not encourage competition between children, and hopes that they do not see themselves as competing with each other. He sees the language itself as the challenge, although his teaching style requires substantial pupil–pupil interaction, and therefore pupils are interested in each other's progress. His comments confirmed pupil opinion that they wished to keep up with the others rather than to beat them. Another teacher welcomed the lack of competitiveness in the earlier stages of GOALS; he found this refreshing, but felt that competition would develop as the work became progressively more difficult at higher levels, and as the range of ability and achievement became more obvious.

One teacher felt that emphasis on success is the whole ethos of GOALS; that teaching is towards success rather than failure. However this teacher encouraged competition:

> The idea is around that you should never discriminate against anybody; there should not be competition in a class, for example, because some will fail. Well if you can show me a better way of getting work done than competition between either different teams, or boys and girls, then I'm very willing to give it a try. I'm all for competition.

However in this case the competitiveness is on a team, rather than an individual, basis. The teacher did not tell individual pupils their class position, but did tell them how many marks they had gained. It was pointed out that different classes differed in their attitudes, and must be handled appropriately.

One teacher expressed interesting views about competition within mixed-ability groups. He had found that pupils in these groups tended to sit according to their abilities, and argued that competition between children of similar abilities was beneficial, but that it could have a negative effect if the bottom pupils compared themselves with the most able. He felt that GOALS, although it is designed on a pass/fail basis could still be used to produce a rank order, and that competition in terms of marks gained is quite possible: 'It doesn't matter in the long run; they'll all end up with the same certificate . . . I think I would rather have some means of showing that the people who were at the top end were there. Otherwise it tends to lose its value'.

At school R, competition is discouraged; the head of modern languages is not in favour of giving students rank order results on their school report forms, and does not do so. Another member of the department argued that not only are graded tests suitable for the wide range of ability in a comprehensive school, but they also fit in with the social theory that competition should not be encouraged because it may lead to an aggressive society. She finds competitiveness across abilities unacceptable, and she also does not issue rank orders. She feels that the GOALS scheme is compatible with her attitude, and encourages pupil cooperation (for example in role-play practice), while strongly decreasing the element of competition since there is a set standard: 'They're not aiming for a vague thing that you've got to be better than everyone else to pass ... You've simply got to be able to do certain defined things, and once you can do them then you get your GOALS certificate.'

GOALS levels 1–3 are intended to demonstrate pupils' language achievements rather than to compare one pupil with another. However GOALS levels 4–5, being CSE and GCE exams, do have a range of grades. The relationship of graded test schemes to the question of competition between pupils is complex, particularly in a scheme such as GOALS, and deserves further study.

Pupil motivation: interest, relevance and other factors

At school R, motivation is affected by 13+ transfer:

> I think certainly the first year we noticed a great increase in motivation from the children coming up from Middle Schools. ... We had found in previous years that they were turned off French; they'd had it more than enough, and really wanted to give up. So certainly the first year, and probably the second year of graded tests, we noticed a change in motivation there, but I would say that for the past couple of years we're slipping back to the situation we were in before where children are fed up with French and willing to get out, and we're almost using the graded tests as a carrot to get them through 3rd year French before they drop out. We never have the same problem with German because it's a new subject to them, and they're excited and interested in it. So one year is fine for an interest, unless they find it very difficult' (teacher).

Another member of the department sees motivation as coming from the communicative approach to language teaching. However, she questions why there should be so much emphasis on testing. She can keep track of progress without the testing, and feels that the tests do *not* give motivation; they can in fact be counter-productive by causing worry. Pupils can be put off the idea of learning languages by becoming bored by parrot-fashion learning, and by the same topics being covered time and time again at subsequent levels. One of her colleagues also argued that GOALS, if not taught properly, can have negative motivational effects: boredom, failure, lack of satisfaction from rote learning without retention. She fundamentally disagrees with the omission of written work.

At school P there were relatively few staff comments on the motivational benefits of a communicative approach to language teaching (as opposed to the GOALS testing structure), and in view of the results of the pupil interviews, it might be that this department rather undervalues such benefits. One teacher pointed out that teaching vocabulary could be very boring, but others felt that relevance was a positive factor, particularly with older children. Another point made was that pupils respond well to talk about the foreign country, in addition to studying the language.

Staff at school Q referred to the possible motivational effects of GOALS-directed teaching, for example by the provision of interesting material, quite apart from the tests and certificates.

> There's no doubt in our view that the GOALS scheme has been a great incentive in languages, and came at a time when it was very much needed, because of the diminishing interest in languages, the diminishing take-up ... I think they've made a significant difference to both the interest in, and the motivation of the young-sters, so far as languages are concerned (headmaster).

The headmaster's support for GOALS on the basis of improved interest in the language was echoed by a staff member, referring to 1st-year classes.

> They're very keen; they're very enthusiastic that they can perhaps go to France for a day and very easily talk French, ask for things in French ... When they've been to France and come back, then you get their reaction: 'They understood what I said, and I actually said "*C'est combien?*" in a shop', and they do feel a sense of achievement.

Motivation is by no means automatic, even in the 1st year, although some pupils will be well-motivated anyway: 'You get children coming in during the first year, the first week, saying "Why do we have to learn French?", so you've got that battle to fight' (teacher). Another teacher felt it would be easier to generate enthusiasm after primary-school French has been phased out. The head of department thought that mixed-ability teaching was a factor, and had found a considerable deterioration in a previous 1st year when setting had been introduced during the year.

One teacher thought his 3rd-year second sets were happier sticking to the text-book, and not doing GOALS. Another teacher, referring to the 2nd year, said, 'Half the class might be enthusiastic and half are bored stiff. "Not GOALS again!" That's some of the reaction.' However the view was expressed that the introduction of GOALS had led to an improvement in discipline with 3rd-year second sets, who could not cope with grammar, provided activities were sufficiently varied during the lesson. This teacher also felt that the GOALS course is sufficiently good to prevent the more intelligent pupils becoming bored. Another was doubtful about disciplinary benefits: 'When you get an excitable class, behaviour can deteriorate very much more quickly, I think, with an oral-type lesson, than with a lesson where you know a certain length of time is devoted always to reading or writing.' It is interesting that in an observed lesson with a 3rd-year second set, the class became much easier to control when oral work was replaced by listening to a tape while referring to a text-book.

A teacher said that he had not heard pupils say anything bad about GOALS, and made the point that the scheme had been used in the school now for three or four years, reducing the possibility of a Hawthorne effect. Others wondered what the effects would be of introducing GOALS more consistently, and extending it higher up the school; perhaps, for example, repetition would lead to boredom. So far there had been little effect on the numbers opting to continue the study of languages in the 4th year, and the head of department was disappointed by that, although there had been a slight increase; he felt that there were other factors, in addition to the introduction of GOALS, which affected the position of languages in the school.

Staff reservations

The principal advantage of GOALS as seen by staff is the change to a communicative approach to language teaching, although a high proportion of oral work is felt to require harder work, and perhaps greater strain, in the classroom. This may be compensated to some extent by a reduction in the volume of marking, and by improved pupil motivation, but it was felt that the introduction of GOALS has led to an overall increase in teacher workload.

Several teachers at school P are finding GOALS harder to teach, or requiring more preparation, than a more traditional syllabus; one expressed reluctance to embark on too many GOALS levels with different years all at once. The large amount of written information provided by the scheme in the form of 'teachers' packs' was not found to be particularly helpful: 'That pack of paper that you just get given, that is really demoralising. You just get given this list of words, and you don't know where to start' (teacher). Another teacher felt that it could be laid out in a much more simple way, having found that a great deal of reading was necessary in order to grasp the details of the syllabuses and the testing structure.

A related reservation held by some, but not all, staff is the complexity of administration.

> Something that I personally feel very unhappy about GOALS is
> that there are lots of bits of paper floating about all over the place,
> and just 'Fill in this' and 'Check that', and the children are supposed
> to have lots of bits of paper, which you do your best to make sure
> they sellotape into their exercise books, but then they lose it, or they
> change exercise books, or it gets orange squash all over it' (teacher).

So much for pupil checklists! But the same teacher stated a justification for
the extra effort: 'You stress to the children how serious it is . . . and so
obviously you've got to have it all sorted out . . . You've got to prepare
yourself very well, and it is demanding . . . But it *is* all worth it.'

With the oral testing, some doubt was expressed at school Q as to what
would happen if the scheme were to be extended in the school not only in
terms of volume of testing, but also as to whether teachers would become
bored with constant testing. There is a certain amount of repetition at successive levels,

> and this interestingly enough was one of the major criticisms of the
> GOALS scheme. Teachers I can remember saying, 'Oh, not again
> the Post Office. They did that for level 1 and now they've got to do
> it for level 2.' 'Yes, but this time they're not posting a letter, they're
> posting a parcel!' (head of dept.).

It was not thought to be realistic to teach items only for recognition at level
1 if they are to be used for production at level 2. The fact that GOALS is a
testing syllabus rather than a course as such, and the lack of a detailed
scheme in French linking GOALS to the text-book, was felt to make
teaching more difficult.

Another factor is period length. School Q operates 55-minute periods,
which may be too long for successful teaching of languages with an oral
emphasis such as is required by GOALS, particularly with younger or less
able children. Long periods also reduce the number of contacts per week.
One teacher argued that one has eventually to come back to doing some
writing, although GOALS levels 1 and 2 contain no writing component.
The need for variety in a 55-minute lesson is clear, and observed lessons
demonstrated this, with use of whiteboards, tapes, video, OHP, text-books
and flash cards, and a range of associated pupil activities. The head of
department particularly recommends the use of role-play in pairs, followed
by exposing some pairs to plenary scrutiny, as a means of breaking up long
lessons while also enabling pupils to practise speaking the language.

The fact that the department has agreed to consolidate the position of
GOALS in the school means that they feel that reservations and difficulties
can be overcome, or that they are outweighed by other factors; there was

overwhelming support for reform of traditional syllabuses, and recognition that a predominantly written course based on translation and grammar is not suitable for modern conditions (if, indeed, it ever was). But enthusiasm for GOALS is tempered by realism; it is certainly not seen as a panacea.

At school R, the head of department is confident that the right decisions have been made in relation to GOALS, but is shocked at the time and effort that have been needed for curriculum development work in modern languages compared with other subjects. She feels that apart from more in-service training in teaching and examining techniques, the department needs more recognition in terms of time and money for the work they are doing.

In-service training

One factor assisting the introduction of GOALS in school P is that several members of the department had some previous knowledge or experience of graded test schemes from their initial teacher training. Another is the key role of the head of department in the development of the scheme; he is therefore particularly able to provide information and advice, as well as communicating his own enthusiasm.

GOALS requires modification of traditional attitudes and practices. At school Q the substantial experience of the modern-languages staff is in many ways an advantage to the department and to the school, but may make it harder to introduce a graded test scheme here than in a department where staff have been trained more recently.

> The biggest and most contentious aspect of introducing it is teacher in-service training, which is quite insufficient. It is felt that teachers join the profession with one set of rules applying in the game, and now another set of rules applies, and teachers have not been equipped to actually handle that change in the rules (head of dept.).

The head of department himself has been a member of GOALS working parties in German and has produced the Lexical Index for level 1, but no one else from the school has been involved in the development of the scheme. Several teachers expressed their lack of confidence in teaching GOALS effectively.

> I think we have taught ourselves the GOALS scheme. It's all there on paper, but in fact in the way we've put it across and so on, it's been very much a matter of trial and error ... The Language Adviser gives us a lot of advice, and we've had meetings and so on, but I think all of us feel that we really would welcome going away

and being trained specifically in the teaching skills of GOALS (teacher).

It is in the communicative style of teaching where further training is felt to be required, not the principles or administration of the scheme. One teacher had found a workshop organized by the county to be interesting and very useful, but others criticized the in-service provision as not satisfying their perceived needs. A session where video films had been shown came in for particular criticism from one experienced teacher.

> I asked (the speaker) at the end of the session why in fact we weren't able to see excellence in these films, and his reaction to that was that there were simply few acknowledged experts in the field around in the country, and yet here we are, totally changing the direction. We are expected by some form of osmosis, or whatever, to suddenly be able to teach to this type of method.

GOALS is clearly regarded as requiring a major change of teaching style, particularly for those whose style has previously been very traditional. A member of staff who is fully committed to the GOALS approach admitted that he continued to be worried about his apparent loss of control over the class when they were doing oral group work.

> I do tend to find that I still want to be the central person in the room, and even if I try consciously not to be, I find that my natural tendency is to drift back to being in control, myself doing the talking, myself guiding them, what they say. I don't know whether that's good or bad. It would appear that for GOALS, you've got to get away from this. You've got to be more lenient, try and accept the fact that it is in control when it may seem not to be.

Pupil opinion

Curriculum

'A major reason for developing the GOALS scheme was to enhance pupil interest, success and motivation' (West Sussex, 1981).

The interviewed pupils had experience both of GOALS and of traditional courses. Almost all were clear about the differences in the lessons, that GOALS puts much more emphasis on speaking and listening, that there is less grammar but a lot of vocabulary, that it deals with relevant, colloquial French or German which would be useful in a practical situation, such as going into a cafe, finding one's way around a strange town, or staying at a hotel. Most liked the stress on conversation, on oral communication: 'You're going to speak more than write. Because when you go to a country, the first thing you do is speak.'

GOALS was thought to be more interesting and enjoyable than a grammar-based course, but a few pupils made comments which confirmed the danger of parroting. 'You just have to learn off by heart what to say in a certain situation. That's so you sort of sound like a tape-recorder if you go over to France or Germany.'

One or two liked GOALS becuase it was different from their previous French course. Some pupils said they felt that they were learning more, and this contributed to their enjoyment. But enjoyment was not necessarily dependent on success, or on the style of course: 'If the teacher makes the lesson fun, then you actually find the subject fun, so it really all depends on the teacher.'

Many pupils' main aim was to obtain as good a grade as possible in their forthcoming public examinations in order to obtain a qualification which would be useful for future employment prospects. From that point of view it did not matter whether they were doing GOALS or not, apart from one or two who thought they might work abroad, or in a job in which they might actually use the foreign language; these pupils preferred GOALS for its emphasis on the spoken language.

This emphasis on speaking was seen by almost all as the principal feature of GOALS. Most liked it, either because they found speaking easier than writing, or because they thought it more useful. However the minority of pupils who disliked GOALS said they did so because *they* found speaking harder. One specific point made was that the speed was too fast, so that they were unable to understand the teacher, or the tapes: 'I've just got one word, just worked out what one word is, and you're on to another whole different sentence.' Another possible disadvantage was embarrassment when they had to speak in front of the class, for example in role-plays: 'Virtually every lesson there's at least one person makes a fool of themselves.'

However, GOALS was praised for encouraging them to speak the language, and practice in the oral tests was argued to be good for their confidence, since 'you get used to talking in front of somebody'. One pupil pointed out that 'everyone's learning: you have to make mistakes to learn, don't you?' Most pupils preferred the opportunity provided by GOALS to speak and understand. One had chosen to do O-level in the GOALS set rather than a higher set for this reason. Some who did not like their language lessons still spoke in favour of GOALS: 'I think it's a good idea to have a course like this, because it is important to learn to speak. I've got nothing against the course; it's a very good course. I just don't like French itself.'

Several pupils said that it was important to have a language; some had included a language in their options because they had been advised to do so, and in one or two cases they were regretting this if they felt they would not achieve good examination results. GOALS was not blamed. 'If I was any good at it, it'd be more useful than the grammar. It'd be a better way of teaching than the other way. But I'm no good at it, so it doesn't really matter.'

Assessment

All the pupils appeared to perceive GOALS primarily as a communicative approach to language teaching rather than as a testing structure.* However many liked the fact that there are tests at regular intervals, which measure their progress as they go along, with the opportunity to retake sections: 'I think that testing is the only way of learning, really.' 'You can't learn it all in a great big load, because you forget some of it, but if you've got little tests you can learn better, I feel.'

The GOALS tests were seen as a definite incentive, and one group realized that there is the possibility of not allowing pupils to proceed if they fail. They favoured this in order to give pupils an aim each year, and to make them work in order to avoid being kept down. One pupil in another group had failed German level 1 in the 3rd year, missing it by one mark, had been very disappointed and felt that it should be possible for a poor performance on one test to be made up elsewhere.

The style of the GOALS tests attracted a lot of support, although some found them quite hard.

I thought it was a very fair and good way of finding out how good you were.

I didn't find them as tests, exactly. I just thought they were enjoyable lessons where for 5 minutes I was outside and I had to talk to the teacher; I didn't think of it as a test. Otherwise I probably would have failed. I hate tests!

Only a few of these pupils had taken more than one GOALS level, but the progressive nature of the scheme was thought to be a good idea 'because then you know where you are in French, what sort of level you're at'. Public examinations were the strongest motivator for some, and others felt that the particular teacher they had was an important factor; several also

*Apart from a pupil in the bottom 4th-year set at school P who defined GOALS as 'different skill levels in French' during an observed period.

mentioned enjoyment of the language. However the GOALS tests are clearly seen as a motivator: 'It'd be a bit humiliating when everyone else passes and you don't.'

The attitude towards competition is interesting. Most do *not* see themselves as competing with others in the sense of trying to do better, and would not wish to do so, but equally there is a strong desire not to be left behind.

> When we went out of the class to be tested, when we come back, everybody's talking: 'Did you pass? What did you get wrong?', and everything. I think that is incentive. When the rest of your mates are getting through, then you want to get through as well. You want to pass it.

At school Q, some were motivated by the GOALS certificates: 'It makes you feel you've achieved something . . . You've actually got something to prove that you've managed to get that far.' However there were difficulties connected with certificates. Quite a lot had failed to complete the GOALS tests for a particular level, or had completed the tests but had not reached the necessary standard; they were not eligible for certificates. In other cases, there had been long delays before certificates had been received, or pupils had not actually received them, although they had satisfied the requirements.* Clearly these factors would be likely to be counter-productive in terms of motivation, although the pupils did not appear to be particularly worried by them.

There were mixed feelings about the certificates at school P. Some said they hadn't known that there were certificates until the end, so for them the prospect of getting one had not been an incentive, although they liked having them: 'I've got a certificate somewhere . . . It shows that I've done a certain standard of German . . . I'm pleased that I've got it.' However another felt that 'It's only a bit of paper', and the group realized that the certificates state what they knew at the time, not necessarily what they remembered. There was doubt whether GOALS certificates would be recognized, or carry weight, with employers. It was felt that what mattered were O-level certificates, and, failing that, CSE.

Overall, the interviewed pupils were in favour of GOALS, would have liked to have done more GOALS, and had few criticisms of the system. Interestingly, two said that there was a danger of becoming bored while oral testing was in progress, and suggested that 'it might be better if another teacher took the test'. The 5th formers at school Q, who were preparing for

---

*This problem should now have been solved by a change in the system for distribution of certificates.

a traditional German O-level, all liked GOALS, but they were unanimous that grammar was also important, and emphasized that just GOALS would be inadequate; their ideal was a course consisting partly of GOALS lessons.

Summary and Conclusions

The case-study schools are all mixed comprehensives, but they cover a range of catchment areas and differ in the age and previous language experience of their entrants as well as in the way language teaching is organized within the school. The way GOALS is used is complex, and is dependent on several factors, including:

- the course structure itself (for example timetabling, setting);
- whether French is started from scratch;
- logistic considerations (particularly oral testing);
- the attitudes of individual staff.

Although there is no clear pattern across or even within schools for the use of GOALS, there are some common features. In all three schools French is compulsory to the end of the 3rd year and the second foreign language is German. By no means all classes are presently involved with GOALS testing, but the three departments are all increasing their commitment to GOALS. Since GOALS does not constitute a course as such it is necessary to integrate the GOALS material with the text-books in use; GOALS content is supplemented with other material, particularly for the more able pupils. GOALS is perhaps seen primarily in terms of curriculum development, as a means to facilitate a communicative approach to language teaching and learning by encouraging a shift towards relevant, useful French and German, and towards speaking and listening as opposed to translation. GOALS represents a substantial change in the content and style of language teaching, although some staff were moving towards a communicative approach anyway: 'I've always believed that language is about communication and not about grammatical rules' (head of dept.).

As well as acting as a catalyst and as a vehicle for the move away from traditional language teaching, other benefits of GOALS include the following.

(1) Potential CSE and O-level candidates can follow the same course, in advance of the introduction of GCSE. The relationship of GOALS to public examinations is an important factor.

(2) Those giving up the study of a language at the end of the 3rd year can be awarded a certificate as a mark of their success and a description of their achievements.

(3) At school R, closer and improved relations with contributing Middle Schools have been achieved.

Principles of mastery learning are not applied to any great extent, and entry for tests on the basis of individual readiness is largely impractical, so that it is difficult to give the intended emphasis to pupil success. It is possible for pupils to be following courses leading to a particular GOALS level without previous experience of GOALS, or having bypassed levels, or having failed at a lower level. In any case levels 4 and 5 cannot be considered in terms of mastery, since being Mode 3 public examinations they have a range of grades rather than a pass/fail division.

However the testing structure is supported, and the GOALS tests are liked by staff, with the provision of short-term aims seen as a benefit (although there may be a risk of over-emphasis on testing). However there are strong reservations about the logistics of individual oral testing, both in terms of the time required and of how to occupy those not being tested. Cover is seen as the only fully satisfactory solution.

Views of staff differ as to whether GOALS-based courses provide a suitable foundation for A-level studies, although some feel that they do; this is to some extent dependent on the particular A-level syllabus taken. At the other end of the ability range there are doubts about whether GOALS can enable all 3rd-year pupils to complete their language courses with a feeling of success. There is the further reservation that GOALS might perhaps encourage too much of a rote learning approach, particularly for weaker candidates. Some staff doubted whether GOALS would enable pupils to reach a point at which they began to use the language creatively.

Support for the GOALS scheme was expressed by the interviewed pupils, who had few criticisms, although some were emphatic that GOALS alone would be insufficient. Most pupils preferred the stress on the spoken language, and approved of the GOALS testing structure. There appear to be several factors which influence pupil motivation. Staff had mixed feelings about possible motivational effects of the scheme and the certificates, although some had noticed benefits in terms of discipline and pupil enthusiasm, at any rate initially. An interesting point arising in the study is the suggestion that a system of assessment based on graded tests might be particularly appropriate in schools where competition between pupils is discouraged, either by the school or by the pupils themselves.

Teachers are finding that a communicative style of teaching is not easy, although there is unanimous support for the principle. Concern was expressed about the complexity of administration and the workload involved in operating GOALS. While there is much support for the GOALS approach, many interviewed staff feel that more resources and in-service training would be needed for it to be operated in a fully effective way. However, in spite of reservations, GOALS is regarded as a considerable advance on traditional language teaching and testing.

Chapter 3

Graded Tests in Mathematics

The Kent Mathematics Project

In mathematics the longest established scheme is the Kent Mathematics Project (KMP), which is a task-based individualized learning programme designed for a wide age and ability range. Case studies were conducted in two schools, X and Y, which have long experience with the scheme. They are both mixed 11–16 high schools (one rural, one urban); at 13+ about 25 per cent of their pupils transfer to upper schools on the basis of 'guided parental choice'.

The Kent Mathematics Project was adopted by the Kent LEA in 1970, after initial development within another of the authority's schools. KMP has some similarities to programmed learning, and Banks (1985) describes the development of the scheme as an application of the principles of educational technology.

There are nine levels, with decimal sudivisons; level 1 is suitable for average 10-year olds and level 9 is rather above GCE O-level. Project materials are now available in published form, and further developments are in progress. KMP consists of a concept framework of topic 'lines' and a material-bank of tasks based on workcards, tapes or booklets, in fast, medium and slow versions where necessary and appropriate. Pupils work at their own pace on individualized 'matrices' of tasks selected from the material-bank. When a matrix is completed a test is taken and a 'corrected attainment level' calculated, which is a measure of pupil achievement and may be used by the teacher to assist in the selection of tasks for the next matrix. Pupils in a class are likely to be working at different levels, and the role of the KMP teacher is diagnostic and tutorial; skills in record-keeping and resource management are also important.

Banks (1985) describes KMP learning objectives as behavioural, and the Teachers' Guide (Kent Mathematics Project, 1978) explains that most objectives describe briefly what the pupil should be able to do after working through the task. However,

> Sometimes, it is more helpful to the teacher, and more concise, to describe the intention of the task in such terms as 'Improve mental skills with tables', which does not describe what the pupil can do after the task but what should happen to the pupil during the task (Kent Mathematics Project, 1978, p. 11).

Items for the material-bank were trialled, and accepted if they satisfied an 80/80/80 criterion, that is 'at least 80 per cent of the teachers considered a task to be at least 80 per cent successful with at least 80 per cent of the students' (Banks, 1985, p. 61).

The scheme does not award certificates, but a Mode 3 CSE has been available through the South-East Regional Examinations Board, and a Mode 2 O-level through the London GCE Board; many other examination syllabuses are also covered by the KMP material-bank. The concept network has evolved over several years rather than being founded on any particular syllabus, and levels have to a large extent been determined heuristically, although they do of course take account of natural progressions in the development of mathematical concepts. KMP is an example of a highly developed and well-established graded test scheme based on individualized learning, and is in use in a large number of primary and secondary schools, both in and outside Kent.

The Teachers' Guide lists project aims.

1. To provide a unique course in mathematics for each individual child, using material suitable for all abilities of children between nine and sixteen years and tailored to pupils' weaknesses and special interests;

2. To provide teachers with a flexible system within which they can, if they desire, introduce their own interests and skills;

3. To give the teacher opportunities to use his or her skills at diagnosing weaknesses, helping children to develop concepts and establishing cooperative rather than teacher-dominant relationships;

4. To provide a system in which children will accept responsibility for most of their own learning, not working in isolation but with social interaction with other children;

5. To offer an assessment of each pupil's mathematical ability at any stage in his or her learning career, culminating in CSE or O-level assessments (Kent Mathematics Project, 1978, p. 6).

It is clear that if these aims are fulfilled, courses based on the KMP material-bank will be very different from traditional approaches to mathematics teaching and learning. KMP is opposed to the 'lock-step' system, under which a set syllabus is covered in a given time. Other major differences are in the changed roles of teachers and pupils, and the changed relationship between them. KMP does not require the teacher to adopt a primarily expository role, but does require the pupil to take an active part in the learning process.

KMP in operation

Operation in the classroom

It is interesting that two schools which are similar in many respects have different policies regarding the place of KMP in the mathematics course structure, with different proportions of KMP periods and different views on the suitability of KMP across the ability range. At school X the proportion of KMP teaching varies, with lower sets doing less. Every set has at least one double period per fortnight of 'traditional' mathematics teaching, and the lowest 4th and 5th form sets do no KMP; these sets study arithmetic only. At school Y the way in which KMP is used has evolved over time; the present situation is that the proportion of KMP periods in almost all sets is between a half and three-quarters. However at both schools, the operation of KMP periods appears in general to conform to project guidelines (see Kent Mathematics Project, 1978).

On entering the room at the beginning of a KMP period, a pupil who is part way through a matrix of tasks must select a card (or sometimes a booklet, or a cassette tape) on which to work, and find it in its box which will be available at the side of the room. If the card is already in use, or perhaps missing, the pupil may select an alternative card from the matrix, or go to another maths room in search of the first card, or consult the teacher. Some cards require apparatus, which again is directly available to the pupils.

When working on a task, if the pupil gets stuck through lack of under-standing or inability to answer a question, s/he may consult the answers on the back of the card, or consult the teacher, or another pupil. When the task is completed, it must be 'signed off' by the teacher, who will ask one or two questions to check genuine understanding, although some teachers will ins-truct pupils not to wait if there is a queue, but to continue with another task, so that sometimes two or three tasks are signed off together.

On completion of the entire matrix of ten tasks, the pupil will ask for a test book, which contains tests on almost all tasks (a few not being suitable for testing), and work through the relevant ones. No assistance from others is permitted at this stage, although some teachers allow pupils to look back at the cards if they need to do so. When the test is finished (for the whole matrix), the pupil hands it in to the teacher to be marked.

It is almost impossible in most classes for teachers to mark tests during the lessons, so if a pupil hands in a test before the end of a lesson that pupil must be kept occupied for the remainder of the time. The KMP system allows for 'free choice' tasks for this purpose, which are usually puzzles or other activities designed to occupy time in an enjoyable but still mathematical way. However these are not used at school **X**, and only to a limited extent for younger pupils at school **Y**. For older pupils,

> I'm afraid the pupils are very keen to get through, to get on, and they tend to look on the free choice as a stop-gap . . . And I would rather that they spent the time working through the KMP system than spending a lot of time on those free choice cards. They consider them a bit of a waste of time (teacher).

The alternative to free choice is to set pupils one or two tasks which will form part of the next matrix while the test is being marked.

The teacher marks the test before the next KMP lesson, and will use the results to diagnose weaknesses, and in designing an appropriate new matrix for the pupil. Pupils will be expected to do test corrections before starting this new matrix, and where weaknesses have been demonstrated the teacher will give the necessary remedial assistance, and perhaps set one or more of the same tasks to be repeated on the new matrix. For each class, a file of records (continuous assessment sheets) is kept by the teacher, including:

(1) the dates on which a matrix is started and completed;

(2) the mean attainment level (MAL) of the matrix, which is the arithmetic mean of the levels of the 10 tasks (each card is assigned to a particular level, always a multiple of 0.2);

(3) the particular tasks set, on a copy of the concept network for each individual pupil;

(4) the test score obtained (x%);

(5) the corrected attainment level (CAL) obtained by the pupil on the matrix, where

$$CAL = MAL - \left(1 - \frac{x}{100}\right) = MAL + (\text{test score as a decimal}) - 1$$

A cumulative set of records is built up for each pupil as they move up the school.

A significant amount of teacher time (outside periods) is needed for marking tests, maintaining records and planning new matrices. Priority tends to be given at the beginning of KMP periods to pupils who have tests to be returned, and pupils with difficulties on tasks in progress are generally helped later. Teachers need also to keep a check on materials, although sometimes monitors are appointed to assist with this (for example by ensuring that all cards are returned to the right boxes).

For the pupil, learning in KMP periods is individual, and comes by reading cards or booklets rather than by listening to the teacher. Compared with traditional learning methods, the pupil is more responsible for organizing his/her own learning, and for ensuring that progress is made, although a skilled teacher will have a system of checks on individual progress through the record-keeping system. When pupils take tests, no particular 'test conditions' operate since tests are taken in the course of regular KMP periods; it is not obvious at a glance which pupils are taking tests in a KMP classroom and which are working on tasks. There will always be a few pupils out of their desks, perhaps obtaining materials, or consulting the teacher, who will spend most of the period giving individual attention of various kinds.

Staff may find KMP periods harder work and more exhausting than class teaching periods.

> To have a quiet KMP lesson is very difficult . . . You're watching all the time to see that they are using it properly. They're coming to you for help, because they don't understand it. They're coming to be 'signed off'; they've finished the card, and you try and look at each card and say 'Anything you didn't understand?', see any mistakes they've made, ask them a question on it. And they come to you, they've finished some work, they've got a test for you to mark . . . It can be very tiring (teacher).

However it was also pointed out that good organization can make KMP less tiring. It is important to manage resources so that pupils can find equipment easily, and to devise methods of reducing the queue of pupils needing attention. Some staff try to circulate round the room during KMP lessons, and this is one way of detecting lack of effort or progress, the other way being through the record keeping system by noticing if a pupil fails to have tasks signed off, or a matrix completed, within a reasonable time. If pupils require a lot of individual assistance, teachers may see them during a lunchtime, or after school, rather than devoting a lot of time to one pupil during a lesson. Sometimes pupils may be able to help one another. The proportion of time spent by teachers sitting at their desks during KMP lessons, dealing with pupils who come to them, as opposed to sorting out problems at the pupils' desks, varies according to the circumstances.

Teachers are aware that Bertram Banks advocated group teaching within KMP periods in order for the teacher to avoid repeating the same bit of instruction with several individuals. However they feel that this would be difficult to implement in practice, the main obstacle being that the remainder of the class would find it hard to carry on their individual work without either needing assistance from the teacher or becoming distracted by the group teaching. It might be possible with an able set, but in practice there is very little group teaching.

Administration of KMP*

At school X it was stated that the department makes a 'conscious effort' to be efficient, and to maintain detailed and accurate records. The importance of keeping up to date was stressed.

> it is absolutely vital that when a test is handed in it is marked almost immediately . . . in preparation for the next lesson, so that they can get on with either a new matrix, or correct the test prior to having the new matrix set (head of dept.).

Therefore the teacher, as well as marking the tests, must plan what action to take with each pupil, and what cards to include on the new matrix, then enter the relevant information on pupil records.

These records are used in the design of new matrices. Colour coding on pupil concept networks makes it possible to see at a glance which tasks have been included in which matrices, and which have been repeated. Although normally new matrices just carry on along the concept lines from where the old matrices leave off, the design of new matrices does offer some scope for teachers to use their skill and experience. Sometimes there are alternatives of different speed or difficulty. Some tasks are dotted on the network, and are optional extras. There are a few cards which particular teachers omit, preferring to cover the ground in a different way in taught periods.

It was pointed out that a single lesson (35 minutes) would be far too short to operate the system in view of the time needed to start the periods, and to clear away at the end. Thus all mathematics at school X is taught in double periods. The resource management role of the teacher is an important one, in order to ensure that pupils can quickly and easily find cards and apparatus, and to minimize the risk of loss or damage. It is also necessary for class discipline to be such that the teacher may devote attention to individual pupils while the remainder are working.

*This section is based on school X. There are some minor differences at school Y.

Taught lessons (non-KMP)

Several reasons were advanced for having at least some non-KMP periods with all sets. For example, taught lessons provide an opportunity for a more thorough treatment of certain topics than is given by KMP. Equally, if a teacher finds particular KMP cards unsatisfactory an alternative approach can be presented in the taught lessons. Such lessons may also be used to tackle difficulties of understanding experienced by pupils in KMP, if these occur frequently in the class. In both schools the department works to a syllabus for taught periods, which is designed to reinforce some of the KMP material, and to supplement it with certain extra topics.

Other reasons that were given for maintaining a mixture of KMP and class teaching periods included:

(1) differing pupil attitudes, with some responding better to classwork, some to KMP, and many responding well to the variety of a mixture;

(2) the danger that some pupils would progress too slowly if all their periods were KMP;

(3) the need for pupils to identify with the group, rather than having purely individual learning;

(4) the difficulty of organising homework when pupils are working on their own;

(5) the reluctance of some teachers to do no class teaching.

It was felt to be essential that mathematics is taught in sets (or bands), so that the KMP range within a group is not too wide for the taught periods. Nevertheless, since pupils work at their own pace on KMP, 'very often some of the group have met what you're talking about and the others haven't . . . But generally speaking, the actual syllabus . . . does tie up with what they've got on the KMP . . . You have to marry the two' (teacher).

Being presented with material twice (in KMP and non-KMP lessons) can reinforce knowledge and understanding. In the case where pupils have covered material in a taught lesson, and then come across it in KMP,

> We say to the children . . . 'If you've got a workcard on something that we've done in class, and you know that you understood it, or you think you did, don't bother to go through the workcard again. Just have a look at the test, and if you can do the test, just do the test and that's it. But if you didn't like it the first time in class, and you find it hard, then go through the card again' (head of dept.).

57

The two teaching approaches can give pupils greater insight, and the staff did not think there was too much difficulty in integrating the content of KMP and class teaching periods, although one teacher found it easier to do a totally different topic in the taught periods rather than attempting to blend with the KMP periods. A teacher at school Y said that their teaching syllabus dovetails very well with KMP. All the staff felt it desirable to have some taught lessons, and were satisfied with the existing balance in their respective schools.

KMP Assessment

Internal assessment at school X

Although the scheme provides an 'entrance test' (KMP, 1978), this has been found to be 'far from adequate' (head of dept.), and school X has designed its own mathematics test of fifty short-answer items. Teachers visit all seven feeder primary schools around June each year, and administer this test to pupils who are about to transfer. The results are used to allocate pupils to first-year mathematics sets, and diagnostically for staff to design appropriate starting matrices for each pupil. Three of the feeder schools do KMP themselves and KMP records from these schools are used in conjunction with the test results. Pupils from other schools do of course require initial training in the KMP system, and assistance in how to operate it, for the first few weeks.

The same entrance test has been found to be reasonably suitable for placing late entrants to the school on an appropriate KMP level (those who transfer in to any year as a result of families moving to the area). However there may be difficulties for such pupils in adjusting to the KMP system.

The KMP Corrected Attainment Levels are used to determine internal assessment grades for all pupils. School policy is for grades 1–5 to be awarded to 10%, 20%, 40%, 20%, 10%(respectively) of pupils across the year group in each subject. In mathematics it is easy to use CALs (which are calculated to two decimal places) for this purpose, there being a wide range of KMP levels across each group. However, there are some problems. For example, the proportion of time spent on KMP varies considerably between sets, higher sets being at an advantage. The head of department, in recognizing this criticism of the grading system, pointed out that movement between sets is possible at any time. The head of lower school was more concerned by possible bias in the grades of pupils who worked on KMP cards in their own time in order to get ahead; it was necessary to be aware of that.

In spite of the use of CALs for grading, the department does set end-of-year examinations

> because we do have pupils who are absolutely bone idle, who do not do as much work as they ought to, and therefore fall back in the KMP level because the work that they do they are finding easy . . . but they're only doing 1 or 2 matrices a year, whereas the donkeys for work are doing 5 or 6 . . . So on our gradings, this potentially intelligent pupil will not come out well, because we've used KMP, but in an exam they normally pull the stops out (head of dept.).

These internal examinations are set for the whole year group, and it is realized that this is not satisfactory in view of the range of knowledge and ability. The head of department would like to find time to set differentiated papers, so that pupils will be examined on what they know, 'but it needs a lot of time to write the exam, and then it'll be a lot more complicated to correlate what is happening in the whole of the year'.

External examinations

The KMP Mode 3 CSE examination is weighted 70 per cent coursework to 30 per cent external examination, with the coursework subject to moderation by visitation. All markers from the twenty or so participating schools attend a meeting to recommend exam grade boundaries to the Board. Coursework grade boundaries are based on the final two CALs obtained by candidates and are determined separately for each school since schools may operate the KMP system differently. The process by which CALs are arrived at is worth further consideration. Its validity depends on the following.

(a) The assignment of KMP tasks to suitable levels. This depends partly on the logical hierarchy of tasks along and between lines in the concept network, and partly on judgments about the relative standards of tasks made by the developers of the KMP scheme.

(b) Acceptance of the principle that the MAL is not in itself an accurate indicator of a pupil's level, and that test scores should also be taken into account; it is also necessary to accept the particular method chosen for converting MALs to CALs.

(c) All candidates within a school having reasonably equal opportunities to obtain high CALs, in terms not only of total available time, but also conditions under which the scheme is operated (for example whether or not pupils are allowed to consult KMP cards during tests).

The method of calculating CALs is accepted by the department as part of the KMP system, and is regarded as a satisfactory way of producing grades for a variety of purposes – internal school assessment, 13+ selection and CSE coursework – although it was pointed out that for diagnostic purposes, test marks on separate KMP tasks need to be considered. An advantage of the CAL is that it is a stable measure of performance, gradually increasing over a pupil's secondary school career and dependent on both ability and effort. As with all forms of coursework assessment it is difficult to eliminate completely the possibility of cheating, and this will be considered in a later section; one safeguard in school X is that factors other than the CAL are taken into account in arriving at candidates' CSE coursework grades. Very few moderation problems are reported to arise with this well-established Mode 3 examination, perhaps another indicator of the validity of the CAL as a measure of mathematics performance.

The KMP Mode 2 O-level also comprises coursework and a final examination, but there are several differences with the Mode 3 CSE, apart from the examination being set by the board. In the O-level, coursework only has 40 per cent weighting and is based directly on KMP Corrected Attainment Levels. CALs are mapped into marks which are added to examination marks, whereas in the CSE *grades* are combined (thus requiring a correction to avoid regression to the mean). In the CSE, coursework material is kept at the school, but is available to the external moderator. In the case of O-level a considerable amount of material relating to the coursework of all individual candidates is sent to the board (flow diagrams for level 6+; test books and records for the last three tests, including marks obtained on each task). There are about twenty schools (600 candidates) entering this Mode 2 O-level; the board reports that moderation is required for a few schools which do not operate the coursework procedures correctly.

The concept of mastery

KMP tests are 'essentially mastery tests' (Kent Mathematics Project, 1981) and at both schools it appears that teachers are applying the principle of mastery learning that pupils have to master tasks before moving on to new material: 'I'm not prepared to let them go on until I'm sure they've understood everything in that matrix' (teacher). However, no particular 'pass marks' or 'mastery levels' are specified, either by the scheme or by the schools. At both schools it is the responsibility of teachers to decide what constitutes mastery, and to attach their own meanings to individual test scores in terms of action to be taken.

> It normally depends on how well they've done in their test. 70 per cent or more, and I would write them out a new matrix immediately of ten cards. If the test is less than 70 per cent then I'm not generally happy with it. I will ask to see corrections, and if the corrections still show weaknesses in certain areas, then those cards will have to be repeated (head of dept.).

Several staff at both schools said that the percentage score on the whole test is less important for diagnostic purposes than the way in which the total score is made up, and how marks have been lost.

It was also pointed out that a particular mark might represent a good performance by one pupil but would be a poor result for another;

> If my top band got under 80 per cent in some of their tests, I will tell them 'You have done very badly. Come on, I expect better work than that.' But if my lower band have got 80 per cent I say 'Well done. I *am* pleased with you' (teacher).

Marks will be interpreted according to the circumstances; what constitutes success may even be negotiable with pupils in some instances. It may be that what really matters is that both teacher and pupil should be satisfied that the material covered in the completed matrix has been satisfactorily grasped, and that the pupil is ready to go on to new work. Several staff stressed that it is important to know the abilities of children well in order to design appropriate new matrices on an individual basis in order to maintain both progress and morale. It was pointed out that consolidation of ground covered is essential, and that there is a danger in KMP of children pushing ahead too rapidly.

Staff also stressed the diagnostic value of KMP tests, and the importance of providing appropriate remedial work; some felt that this aspect of KMP should be emphasized more to the pupils. One teacher said that low test scores were often caused by a pupil missing one major point, or failing to understand the wording of questions, and that such difficulties can usually be cleared up very quickly. She would be very worried if pupils did not get sufficiently high marks on tests, because it would mean that they are not working at the right level.

Policy regarding test corrections varies, but at least one teacher always requires corrections to be done before pupils start work on a new matrix. There is sometimes difficulty if pupils are asked to repeat a card, and still fail to master it. There is no point in asking for the card to be repeated indefinitely, and one teacher said that she would never tell pupils to repeat a card on the next matrix, since that would be soul-destroying, but would always find some alternative. It was suggested that the KMP system might be improved by the provision of extra practice material at each level. One of the aims in class lessons is to give further practice in, and revision of, topics covered in KMP; in cases where the KMP treatment is not felt to be satisfactory an alternative approach can be presented in class lessons: 'If you find a whole lot of them are having a problem on a particular topic it's usually only something that a quick bit of blackboard work will help with.' It might be assumed that experience with the KMP system helps staff to assess mastery, to diagnose and remedy weaknesses, and to make use of other resources as appropriate.

Suitability of KMP across the ability range

Views and policies in departments X and Y

There can be a spread of two or three KMP levels within a class, and this could pose problems for the class teaching periods, but in practice these do not appear to be serious. Teachers pitch their lessons at the median, or rather above that, with some special attention for the weakest members of the set. Again, it can help for a topic to come up a second time on a KMP task. As far as the KMP periods themselves are concerned, the range of ability does not matter, although it can be demanding on the teacher who may have to give assistance on several topics at different levels in quick succession.

With the exception of the weakest 5th-year set, KMP is used right across the ability range at school Y, which is fully comprehensive in Years 1 and 2. In general it is felt to be suitable for all pupils, although it was pointed out that (for example) level 3 is easy, with high test scores obtained, for the upper band 1st year, but harder for the lower band 3rd year. There are some doubts about the system for weak pupils.

> I have some reservation about the effectiveness of KMP with some of the lower-ability group. I think one of the basic flaws with KMP is it's something of a skiver's charter. We work a very tight ship here, in that I not only keep my KMP folder records up to date, but I have a mark book that I enter tests in with dates, so that I can see over the continuing year just how many matrix the pupil is getting through. But on the other hand it's very difficult to turn round and say to a pupil 'You should be working harder', because of course the whole idea of KMP is they're working at a pace that suits them (teacher).

Another teacher argued that the weakest pupils often lack the necessary concentration, self-discipline and reading ability to cope with KMP. An attempt is made in the school to make KMP less daunting for low-ability children by giving them fewer tasks (say six or seven) on a matrix. The Kent Mathematics Project has produced L material designed specifically for slow learners, and this will be discussed in the next section. Set size is a problem in the operation of KMP with academically weak pupils, and another difficulty for these pupils is the tests, which they may be unable to do: 'If you tell them the answer you are defeating the object; if you don't tell them the answer then they will be on that task for ever after' (teacher). If such pupils are set tasks on lower levels, there is the risk that the material will be too childish.

At the other end of the ability spectrum there appear to be no problems with KMP, and the system is thought to work well with the brightest children at both schools.

A teacher said he regrets losing the most able pupils at the end of the 2nd year, and envisages 'people on KMP being able to take an O-level, say at the age of 14'. Another teacher pointed out that KMP is very suitable for pupils who are able at mathematics, but do not transfer to upper schools because of their performance in other subjects; KMP allows such pupils not to be held back. However, none of the upper schools has seen sufficient advantages in KMP for able pupils to introduce it themselves!

The KMP L-materials

The 'L' materials (Limited language) are intended for 11–16 year old pupils in approximately the lowest 15–20 per cent of the ability range (Cole, 1984). These materials have been tried at school X. However they have found that pupils still have difficulty reading the cards on level 1L, and require more time for individual attention and assistance than the teacher has available. One teacher praised some of the material on level 2L, and the head of department found it useful to combine some L material with the ordinary cards in order to extend the range of cards that slow pupils can attempt, and provide extra practice, particularly on number work. However he finds that there is 'no real comparison between a level 2L and a level 2 on difficulty of content', which causes problems in the validity of MALs calculated from combined matrices. Overall, it is not felt in this department that the L material makes KMP suitable for bottom sets. On the other hand at school Y some (but not all) staff feel that the L material is very good, and copes with some of the reading difficulties experienced by the weak sets.

In an evaluation of the introduction of the L materials into five Bedfordshire schools, Cole (1984) found that teachers felt comprehension and readability levels to be suitable for pupils with learning difficulties.

> The learning tasks were considered appropriate to the level of understanding of pupils, offering a variety of learning experiences and methods of presentation. The materials were found to be particularly interesting and motivating for the pupils, although the enthusiasm of teachers using them may well have radiated, causing some of this effect (Cole, 1984, p. 35).

However, it was stressed that the materials were found to be most effective with smaller groups of pupils. Cole (1984) reports that inadequate reinforcement of learning was a weak point of the materials, and that all the surveyed teachers were using other materials as well to assist in the mastery of concepts. On the positive side, there were beneficial effects with regard to pupil attitude resulting from involvement in the administration of their own learning.

Staff Opinion on the Impact of the KMP

Advantages and disadvantages of KMP

The Headmaster of school Y sees many advantages in KMP.

> it allows children to succeed, not just in terms of the classroom Mathematics that goes on, but they can see that there are incentives built into the Kent Mathematics scheme which allow them to be responsible for their Mathematical education.

Other advantages of KMP from the headmaster's perspective are that it assists the process of giving information and guidance to pupils and their parents and that it promotes continuity of learning from primary to secondary level. At the same time it enables children

> to retrace steps, and to go back to the beginning, and to be very much involved with that, rather than to be going on with a sense of guilt that they don't understand something that they've never understood, and not able to get it right . . .

Overall, he feels that 'it's an incredibly good way of giving children opportunities in maths rather than just creating hurdles for them'.

However, the headmaster has several reservations about the KMP system. For example, some pupils may fail to ask teachers for assistance when required, and there are doubts about long-term retention of material. He does not regard KMP as the total answer to mathematics teaching in the school, and fully supports a proportion of class teaching. He dismisses the idea that KMP might be in some way 'teacher-proof', and argues that it requires skilful operation.

> it is a scheme that could in fact become, through poor organization in the school, a meaningless set of activities for children. In the hands of teachers who are really understanding the opportunities that it gives for a consultative approach rather than the straight-forward chalk and talk, the opportunity to provide individual incentives for children, then it's a super scheme.

The Head of Department Y sees the main advantage of KMP as its ability to deal with children who learn at different rates, and quoted the American psychologist, Carroll.

> He says that aptitude is really the amount of time that someone takes to master a particular task ... So I think the whole thing about KMP is making sure that every child makes progress, and just acknowledging that it will be different for every individual.

The capacity of KMP to respond to the abilities and efforts of individual pupils by permitting differential pacing was stressed by other staff at both schools.

> I like KMP right the way through, for all the years, because I think then they are able to get on at their own speed and they're not held back ... Equally with the slower ones, they're not under any pressure to keep up with the rest of the class, as they are in a taught lesson (teacher).

Other reported specific advantages are that it enables pupils who haven't understood something in a class lesson to try again on an individual basis with a KMP workcard, and that problems caused by missing periods through absence (for example as a result of illness, or work experience) are minimized. KMP provides clear targets for pupils which since they are set individually can always be within their grasp. KMP has other effects on the learning process.

> A possible advantage (I'm not sure if it is or not) is that sometimes the cards leave it up to the kids to make a jump from one step to the next step; it's not always obvious. Sometimes they come out with a card, and they ask you 'How do I get from here to here?', or 'What

does this mean?' Sometimes they do it themselves, and so I presume that, having worked it out for themselves, they're going to remember it better. They understand it better if they have been able to do it on their own (teacher).

But the same teacher felt that methods of doing things found by the pupils themselves might not be suitable for future work, for example, in algebra. The teacher, on the other hand, would show them methods which 'will stand them in good stead for when they come up against something a bit harder later on'. It could be that 'if they are left to their own devices, and they're not really being given practice on setting things out . . . they might be developing bad habits for the future' (teacher). Another teacher also cited the tendency of pupils to produce just a string of answers, with no working shown, as a reservation about KMP. This might be another good reason for having some non-KMP lessons, where good setting-out of work can be emphasized.

The variety of tasks within a matrix is another feature of KMP; it can lead to loss of continuity in learning: 'To follow the KMP system necessitates that one year they're going to do the beginning of a topic, then they have to wait for the next year to get on a higher level so that they get the next instalment' (teacher). He quoted the topic of 'Transformations' as an example; this occurs on level 2 but not again until the end of level 4. Taught lessons could be used not only to give a more thorough treatment than the cards provide, but also to tie up loose ends and assist better continuity of learning.

Generally, staff are happy with the content of KMP tasks, although there was criticism of some cards where teachers feel that the treatment of the topic is unsuitable because they dislike the approach, or the wording is unclear, or there are insufficient examples. 'You really want a monitoring system via schools, to pick up cards that are worded badly' (teacher). Overall the mathematics staff all support KMP, although they are aware of the drawbacks.

One teacher had come to do KMP with strong misgivings, feeling that there were loopholes in the system where pupils could cheat, and that there was a place for old-fashioned methods which would ensure that pupils learned. However she now feels that KMP is very suitable for a school where there is a wide spread of ability within maths groups, that it keeps the pupils interested and happy, and that it gets the best out of most children. She mentioned one problem of KMP, that pupils who transfer in from other schools sometimes find it difficult to adjust.

The testing structure of KMP is supported by the staff. The tests serve a monitoring function, enabling teachers and pupils to keep track of progress, and whether material is being assimilated satisfactorily. KMP records give a teacher who is taking a group for the first time knowledge of the ability of each pupil, which is updated at each subsequent test.

Pupil motivation

A range of views were expressed by staff on this issue. On whether pupils prefer the KMP or the non-KMP periods, the teacher who is new to school X said:

> I haven't yet found a child who prefers the ordinary, taught, traditional-style maths . . . They like it [KMP]. I don't know why they like it. Whether it's because they can get on and work on their own, and they prefer to do that, and they prefer to discover their own methods of solving things, or . . . because it means the teacher is off their back and they can escape into their own world, I don't know.

But a teacher with longer experience of the system said:

> Some pupils don't like it, because they think they've got to work harder in the KMP lesson, because there's no teacher working for them . . . Some would be the other way round, because I think some of them, again possibly the brighter ones, feel that in a traditional lesson they're being held back, because they know it, but the teacher's still explaining it on the board because of those that don't know it, whereas in KMP they're not waiting for anybody else; they're going at their own speed.

It was also pointed out that some pupils may like KMP periods because of the opportunity provided *not* to work hard! 'You get the less motivated students put the brakes on. It's less easy to check what they're doing, and therefore it's easy to slide' (teacher).

If a time limit is set for matrix completion, learning is no longer completely self-paced, but pupils know what was expected of them. Less able pupils might be set reduced matrices, say of only five cards, in order to provide a realistic goal. The most able pupils would be free to go faster; they are probably well-motivated in any case, but it was argued that KMP could reinforce that motivation.

> I think the system . . . actually caters for their desire to get on, and their desire to find out more. So they're not dependent on waiting for the rest of their class to reach their level, or they're not feeling

> that they're holding the rest of the group up. They have total freedom to go at their own pace, which I think is good (teacher).

So KMP is sufficiently flexible to cater both for pupils who can pace themselves, and those that need the teacher to pace them. The possible danger that the first group might rush through the material too fast was thought to be covered by the KMP testing system. At school X it was argued that weaker sets tend to be less motivated anyway, and that KMP can produce frustration rather than positive motivation for weak pupils. Motivation is seen as an important factor with KMP, as with any method of teaching and learning, but not as necessarily created by the system itself. 'The system only works as long as the student remains motivated. They've . . . got to provide the motivation themselves, to do the cards. And they've got to push themselves. And the bright kids do' (teacher). The fact that KMP is *not* seen as having motivational advantages for the less able pupils was given as another strong reason for reducing the proportion of KMP for those pupils.

Several staff emphasized the importance for motivation in KMP of setting tasks at a level appropriate to the individual. Pupil confidence was also felt to be important, especially for junior pupils — confidence in the mechanics of the system (for example, operation of cassettes), confidence in their ability to tackle the questions, and confidence in the content of the cards: 'they lost a bit of faith when they found that two of the answers on the cards were wrong' (head of lower school). If confidence is lacking then the teacher is likely to be plagued with (perhaps unnecessary) questions.

At school Y several motivational advantages of KMP were stated by staff. KMP sets clear targets which are within the capabilities of pupils, with emphasis on confidence and success; the provision of tasks of realistic difficulty levels is seen as a key feature. The KMP testing procedures contain incentives, to obtain high scores or to reach a higher level. While the scheme does not award certificates, several teachers offer extrinsic rewards in the form of chocolate bars to pupils who achieve defined criteria, for example a test mark of 100 per cent, or an improvement of 15 per cent or more. Teachers feel that some pupils dislike class teaching and prefer KMP lessons because of the opportunity to work on their own, at their own pace. The intrinsic interest of the material in some of the KMP tasks was also mentioned, although this does not seem to be regarded as a major motivating factor.

> It's a much freer atmosphere with KMP, but they tend to work well in it. I think they enjoy choosing their work as well . . . My 2nd year group, if they've got construction cards, or puzzle cards, they'll do those first, and generally they leave things like algebra, and base numbers, directed numbers till last (teacher).

It seems to be generally agreed that it is harder to motivate the 4th and 5th year lower band groups. 'Most children love KMP. You'll have the odd one or two children in each group who don't. The older ones sometimes say they are bored' (teacher). They may be bored with KMP or with mathematics in general. Variety is regarded as an antidote to boredom, and staff feel that many pupils like a mixture of KMP and class teaching. However there is a range of views. One teacher, referring to a low 5th-year set, said:

> They work much harder on KMP than they do in class lessons . . . They do not like class lessons, because they've got to keep up with you, and they've got to write as you talk. And if there's something on the board that they need, they have got to concentrate on it and do it then, whereas with KMP, if they switch off for a minute or two they haven't lost anything, so actually they much prefer KMP. But I don't think it motivates them particularly well; I think they're more likely to get somewhere with KMP than they are with anything else.

She finds this group 'well-behaved and not too bad' provided she does not try to make them work too hard. A contrasting view about the relative merits of KMP and class teaching for older pupils was given by another teacher:

> Some children . . . respond more to class teaching, I think. Individualized teaching is not a major force for a lot of children, especially I find the older children. The younger children seem to be very well motivated. They want to please, and they want to get on, they want to get to the higher level. The self-competition is good enough for them, also the competition with their friend as well. But when it gets to the older ones, who often lack a lot of motivation, I think a class lesson, you've got them all there, you can pick them out more, and I think you can teach them more.

One teacher argued that some children will work whatever the system, and others will *not* work whatever the system unless they are forced to do so. She sees KMP as 'an opportunity for the well-motivated bright child to go ahead'. KMP records provide evidence for teachers to chase up pupils who they feel should be working faster.

It was thought that competition could act as a motivating factor with able pupils, not in terms of test scores, but in terms of matrices completed and who is going to be first onto the next level.

Differing opinions were expressed on this question of competition between pupils. One view is that KMP encourages healthy competition to reach higher levels, although not all pupils respond to this, and 5th years in particular are more concerned with their personal examination grades and less interested in the performance of others. Another view is that competition is best regarded as being against individual goals rather than against each other: 'I don't hold one up against the other . . . because that's not the point of the system. The scheme is to encourage everyone at their own level' (teacher).

Possible abuse of the system

Staff are aware of several ways in which it is possible for pupils to abuse the KMP system. The first is for a pupil to regard KMP periods as an opportunity to do little or no work. This danger can be minimized by teachers' use of their KMP record books to monitor pupil progress, and at school Y it was pointed out that whereas in class lessons pupils may not be able to get away with wasting time, in KMP they cannot get away with over-reliance on the teacher. KMP provides an opportunity for pupils to take responsibility for their own work which may be rarely available elsewhere in the curriculum, but perhaps this cannot be achieved without risk of abuse.

A second possibility is for pupils to copy answers from the back of the workcards without working through the card in any thorough way. 'It's a matter of maturity, isn't it. You're going to have to explain to them that they are defeating the object, but invariably you do catch them cheating, looking at the answers before they actually do the question' (teacher). One or two teachers think that it might be better to have separate answer books (as is done with SMP), but cheating on cards is not thought to be a serious problem by staff, although it is an issue often raised by parents at open evenings: 'Most of the pupils here tend to have quite a mature attitude. The school's drummed it into them that you're only cheating yourself by looking at the answers' (teacher).

Sometimes 5th-year pupils are tempted by exam pressure to copy answers, but it is felt that most pupils do use the answers in a sensible way, to check their work. Teachers can check that cards have been properly worked through at the signing-off stage.

> Pupils should have their workcards signed off fairly often and should not be allowed to leave a lot of workcards to be signed off in one go. Try to make time to ask one or two questions about the workcard. If anyone seems to be just writing the answers down, and working out is noticeably missing, make them do the card again (Department notes, school Y).

However pressure of time, and the wish to avoid long queues, make this advice difficult to apply in every case.

Any cheating on cards should, of course, be detected when pupils take end-of-matrix tests. However there are also ways of cheating on tests, which are more than usually difficult to supervise in KMP, since they are done on an individual basis during ordinary lessons, with different pupils taking the same test at different times. Cheating does sometimes occur, and the Head of Department X is well aware of the possibility of cheating on tests.

> There are some that may try and cheat the system, but not normally on doing the cards. The problem that we have more than any other is that they tend to try and cheat on the testing, and you have to be very aware that they've not got someone's test book ... open in front of them. If we had more shelf room, then we would take away the pupils' KMP test books ... Unfortunately the administration and the amount of room that we would need to do it is prohibitive.

He felt that it is a small but significant problem. At school Y, test books *are* locked away when not in use, so that pupils cannot usually copy test answers directly from others who have done the same test. This reduces, but does not eliminate, the problem.

> I wouldn't say they can never cheat at all, because I think they can, but then you get them cheating in formal conditions, they'll copy from someone who's better. I don't think it's any worse in KMP ... I don't regard it as a problem, because I think your experienced KMP teacher will pick it up (teacher).

It was also pointed out that the smaller the size of the group, the easier it is to prevent abuse of the KMP system.

Staff motivation and in-service training

The extra administrative load on the teacher due to operating KMP is balanced to some extent by the fact that no preparation is needed for KMP periods, once the teacher is familiar with it. Workload appears to be a potential, but not an actual, demotivator. Several teachers stressed the importance of KMP record-keeping. 'You can have 30 children all doing different things, tests finishing at different moments, different levels, and if you don't record carefully and keep up to date, then it's just chaos in the end' (teacher). It appears that staff are sufficiently well-motivated, and have sufficient faith in the KMP system, to put in the necessary effort, which can lead to a sense of satisfaction in pupil achievement. Staff morale may also be encouraged by the unanimity of approach created by operating KMP.

The KMP lessons are found satisfying and enjoyable by some teachers. However, not all teachers said they prefer KMP teaching, and negative points mentioned were loss of contact with pupils, as compared with class teaching, and less control over their learning. It is possible for the teacher to feel redundant at times in a KMP period, when pupils are working without needing any help, and not appreciating a teacher looking over their shoulder, although at other times the teacher would be harassed with questions. One member of department Y said that KMP denies the teacher the satisfaction of presenting a well-prepared lesson (although there is still the opportunity for that in the non-KMP periods). Several staff argued that it helps considerably to be a maths specialist.

> I think some children think the staff have an easy time in a KMP lesson . . . but you've got perhaps a queue of 6 of them, and they all want different topics, and so you've got to be able to switch your mind quickly. So I think you would need to be a mathematician to work it (teacher).

However one teacher felt that the KMP cards are sufficiently self-explanatory for a maths specialist not to be needed with junior classes. All staff said that they support the mixture of the two types of period, and there is the point that if the school only did KMP it might be difficult for a teacher to move to a non-KMP school.

The headteachers of both schools said that in-service training is encouraged, to increase effectiveness and to promote staff morale. The Head of Department X feels that access to advisory support is useful, and mentioned positive support for KMP from the local authority, for example in organizing regular area meetings for teachers. The LEA also organizes three-day residential courses for teachers new to KMP. Staff are encouraged to attend and the courses are seen as very useful. At school Y, the probationer had done the course in October, and felt that before that his operation of KMP had been rather hit and miss, although he had received a lot of advice and help from other members of the department.

> We looked at KMP from a beginner's point of view, so we went through setting up KMP, looking at different levels, use of cards, philosophy behind the KMP system . . . mock setting of work, given a particular matrix and a child on a particular level, and developing the work with the child, looking at the test scores, analysing what needed reinforcement, and making up a new matrix, which I found very useful . . . Very valuable indeed (teacher).

He regards KMP as 'a nice introduction to teaching' since not too many classwork lessons have to be prepared and presented, and KMP materials provide not only a source of ideas but also help the new teacher develop a sense of grading.

Pupil Opinion

Learning from KMP material

A very wide range of views was expressed by the pupils. Many can see both advantages and disadvantages in KMP, and like having a mixture of KMP and class teaching, but there are some who would like all their periods to be KMP, and some who would prefer no KMP at all. Several of those interviewed had joined the school later than the 1st year; some of these, but by no means all, had found difficulty in adjusting to KMP.

Some pupils like learning from the KMP cards.

> It's quite easy to understand, because it's well set out . . .

> The good thing about it is you're just given a card and you might never have heard of it before, but you're set to do it, and so that way you can learn . . . Then afterwards you're given a test to do, after you do the whole ten [tasks], so you have to remember what you've done . . .

> at the top of the card it says objectives, doesn't it, and I think that's good, because if you read it and find out what the objective is . . . then you go through the card and you make sure you learn the objective. And if you've learnt that, then you've succeeded, I think.

But other pupils think they learn more from a teacher, and prefer to learn that way. They find it hard to learn from the KMP cards because of confusing wording or insufficient explanation, or because they find it hard to concentrate.

> if the teacher is standing there teaching you, and writing things on the board, I think I learn much more that way. I think a lot of people do.

> [KMP] doesn't explain it . . . It asks you really difficult questions, and doesn't go through it with you stage by stage. That's the part I dislike about it. Then you've got to go to the answers and work out your own method back, or go up to the teacher . . .

> If you don't feel like working that day, you can just dream the lesson away and not really do anything in it, and still make it look like you've done something, but if you're doing traditional maths, we get homeworks and that, and we really do learn. I find I learn much more by traditional than KMP

It is recognized that there are other differences between KMP and a taught course besides learning by reading cards as opposed to learning by listening to a teacher. One pupil argued in favour of a mixture of KMP and non-KMP periods on the grounds that in KMP a wider range of topics is covered, 'but you don't go into everything in so much detail as you do in traditional'. Many others like a mixture of systems, and it is realized that there can be advantages in covering a topic in both KMP and taught periods.

> Purely KMP I wouldn't like, but . . . we have two class lessons and two KMP lessons. It works out if I do something in a class lesson and I don't get it fully I go along in KMP and then I understand it fully by going through the cards

This pupil was one of those who thought they can understand things more quickly when taught orally by a teacher than by reading a card. If they do understand fully from the teacher, they do not work through the card when it comes up on KMP but go straight to the test; this saves time and prevents any possible boredom through repetition of material. Sometimes it happens the other way round, with a topic coming up first in KMP and then in class, but this also received favourable comment. Pupils like the teacher to explain things again, perhaps in a different way to KMP, and the teacher's explanation will be easier to understand if the topic has already been encountered in a KMP task. Those pupils who like a mixture of the two types of period find the balance about right, and that what they do in each fits together reasonably well. One group said that their teacher sometimes tells them to omit parts of KMP tasks when she has used a different treatment. Overall there was a difference of opinion between those who feel they learn more in class lessons and others who feel they learn more in KMP. One girl who prefers class teaching realized that if all periods were on that, she might wish she was back doing some KMP!

Variety in the cards forming a KMP matrix, and choice in the order in which they are tackled, are appreciated by many pupils, who do not find the variety confusing. However others took the opposite view, arguing that KMP suffers from lack of continuity, with insufficient time spent on each topic before moving to another.

The level of difficulty of the material is thought to be within most pupils' grasp; they can usually understand it given that the teacher is available to provide help when required. One or two pupils feel that the cards are insufficiently durable. Booklets were criticized because of excessive length, and tapes also attracted some adverse comment. 'What I don't like is when you have to do the cassettes, because I get all in a muddle with the cassette and the tape recorder and the ear phones; it takes so much time.' Free choice tasks are disliked by those few who commented on them. 'If the teacher gives you something, then you know it's going to be part towards your syllabus . . . I don't like free choice.'

Several pupils suggested ways in which they thought KMP, regarded as a material-bank, could be improved. Some would like more practical work, and several mentioned work connected with computers.* One, who had found that level 3L explained things easier than level 3, favoured making the explanations simpler and easier to understand. Another wanted *less* explanation at level 6 and above.

> On the higher levels they could cut down the cards just to the facts
> that the people need . . . They still treat you as though you've got a
> real numb brain that can't understand all the complicated words . . .
> At the lower levels you just need encouraging into it, and if it's easy
> to understand then so much the better.

There is a wide range of pupil opinion on the relative merits of KMP and class teaching in terms both of enjoyment and of learning mathematics. The major points on which there might be consensus are that variety is liked, and that pupils often find that understanding is improved by covering ground twice, although not by mere repetition.

Working at one's own pace

One of KMP's main strengths for the pupils is its ability to cope with different rates of progress within the same class:

> I prefer KMP, because you can work at your own pace; you don't
> have to struggle to keep up, or wait around for people to catch up.

> The teacher can sit down, and get on with specific people that the
> teacher wants to help, and the other people can get on and do their
> work.

*In an observed period, a computer was in use, but with non-KMP material. KMP periods seem very suitable for the situation where there are thirty children but only one computer.

KMP enables pupils to be to some extent independent of the teacher. 'If you're doing KMP and you haven't got a teacher, you can just get on with it, but with traditional maths you can't; you have to wait for another stand-in teacher.' Equally, pupils can miss a lesson, and carry on where they left off.

Working at one's own speed can aid understanding, but it is realized that KMP provides opportunities for slacking, and wasting time: 'It doesn't exactly push you. Unless you're interested in it you don't work.' But not all agree: 'We've got a good enough teacher to stop us from sitting there doing nothing.'

Some pupils have learnt to pace themselves well, and like organizing their own work.

> I think it's important to get a good test mark, and to actually, when you do a card, make sure you know what you're doing and you go through it thoroughly, not to just rush through it . . . But at the same time keep a good line of cards flowing into the teachers, to be marked off.

Setting a time-limit for the completion of matrices is one way in which teachers can attempt to reduce slacking by pupils, and this may be a satisfactory compromise between teacher control and pupil freedom of pace, although it may lead to tasks being completed in a less than thorough way, in order to meet a deadline. For exam pupils, another possibility is to specify the level to be reached by a given date if pupils are to be entered for O-level, but this does not appear to be entirely successful.

> The idea [of KMP] is good. Instead of just getting bored with the teacher you can sit down and do it at your own pace. The trouble is, because we can do that, it's not taken seriously . . . Because we have to get to a certain level . . . so we just rush to get to that level . . . You don't go through it slowly and do all the cards, you just go and do the tests, and try and get the answers, and you don't really learn anything by it.

Nevertheless, for some pupils, pace of working is undoubtedly influenced by the incentive of aiming for a particular coursework grade. Another possible factor is competition with others, although this does not always apply: 'The choice is yours. You can either work at your own pace or race against other people.'

In summary, pupils mostly like the idea of working at their own pace, and can see its advantages. But they can also see its drawbacks, and in practice many of them do not work as hard in KMP periods as in class periods.

The principle of having tests at the end of each matrix received a great deal of support.

> I think it's good where you've got a test on each level, as the cards get harder . . . So if you can't do some particular thing, you repeat the card, and then you get the hang of it gradually, as you go along.

> You have to have a test, just to see that you've remembered it.

The tests are generally felt to be fair.

> I like them, because they go into all the things you've done on a card, and you can't look at the answers as you can with a card . . . I think the tests are good, because they're a good reflection of what's been said on the card.

A few pupils criticized unevenness of standard within a level, but others felt the difficulty of the tests is about right.

Several said that they find it difficult to remember material on the cards when they are taking the test. It was pointed out that since they don't take notes in KMP, it is difficult to revise for tests; this was regarded as a disadvantage of the system. Several pupils said they sometimes need to refer back to the cards during a test.

The method of arriving at the CAL seems to be accepted, and many pupils thought it good for coursework grades to count towards public examination results: 'There are some people who are better at coursework than tests [exams], and others who are better at tests than coursework . . . It's not biased towards any particular people . . . So there's fairness in it. It's a great system.' One pointed out that the inclusion of KMP coursework could disadvantage bright but lazy candidates, while boosting the results of others. Another said that some pupils start off with an advantage by being on higher levels when they first come to the school.

In the case of the 5th-form O-level set (school Y), the way in which KMP is used has been modified.

> Before, we used to all work through a matrix and then we'll do the test. But when you get to the end of the syllabus you've covered so much of the maths that really you just need to flick through the card, just refresh your memory, and then you can go through and do all the tests, without really looking at the cards, because you already know the maths from the classwork lessons.

In fact the KMP tests are sometimes used as a diagnostic tool to find out whether the pupil needs to work through the card. One or two pupils (from both 4th- and 5th-form top sets) dislike doing KMP for O-level. These pupils thought that all their mathematics learning could be done in class lessons, and that the KMP lessons were merely seen as a means of reaching the required standard for the O-level coursework grade. However, other pupils were quite happy with the way the system operates, although some were perhaps reluctant to admit this:

> I've got no grumbles about it. Of course there's the teacher–pupil hate relationship all the time, which is expected to a certain degree, I suppose. But I've got no actual complaints about the course; I think it's good.

Motivation and competition

Many different motivating factors were mentioned by pupils. Some are motivated by mathematics as a subject, with enjoyment mediated either by its perceived importance or by their success in it. One of those who like maths thinks that KMP itself encourages effort, 'because just normal maths lessons get so boring'. Others who do not like maths find KMP the least bad. Enjoyment was said by several pupils to be a motivator, but others think that it is teacher pressure that makes them work. These pupils often prefer class lessons to KMP, although they may also like the freedom of a KMP period: 'I enjoy doing KMP, but it's not doing me any good.'

Almost all pupils regard mathematics as a useful and important subject, and some pupils felt that whether they were doing KMP or not made no difference to their motivation. Those who commented on whether they worked harder in KMP or non-KMP periods were divided in their views, although some felt that they were not pushed hard enough in KMP: 'In the end it's only for your good, isn't it, to be given more homework and to be pushed on. Well I think it is.' Perceived lack of relevance in the KMP material can be demotivating, as can difficulty in understanding the cards: 'I know you can go up to the teacher, but sometimes you feel a bit stupid, keeping going up all the time.' One had liked KMP initially, but not subsequently: 'I think in the first year, it was just a novelty, to start doing something different to normal maths. But then after a couple of months it just wore off, and I just didn't like it really.'

Since many of the pupils interviewed were preparing for public examinations at the end of the year, it is not surprising that these were stated to be a major motivating factor, to provide a qualification for further education or to enhance employment prospects: 'If I didn't want the exam I probably wouldn't try at all.'

Many do not see themselves competing with other pupils, but are concerned simply with their own performance, and work at their own pace, trying to reach higher levels: 'I don't see myself in competition, because all I've got to do is try and get the best grade I can in maths . . . It doesn't bother me what other people are getting . . . in KMP.' However others feel that there is an element of competition: 'you're trying to outdo others . . . trying to get ahead of them . . . to a higher level'. Some compete, but only against particular individuals:

> Me and a friend went up onto level 7 about the same time. We race to compete, see who can get to level 8 first. I think that's good, because it speeds you on. You think 'I'm going to learn this quicker', and so you get more done . . . and at the same time there's an element of fun in it.

It seems that what KMP level someone is on is much more important than what test marks are scored, although pupils may be interested in their friends' scores. Seeing others reaching a higher level can make some pupils work harder in order to keep up, or catch up, but equally getting in front can make them ease off: 'I reached level 7 before a lot of the kids, and when I got there, the first couple of weeks I didn't really do much, because I'd reached the standard.'

Pupils are told what KMP levels are needed for particular coursework grades. This has the advantage of providing clear goals, but again there is the possibility that they may sit back once they have reached the desired level.

Although attitudes vary, competition with other pupils does not appear to be a major motivating factor. In fact no clear pattern emerges; it seems that different pupils are motivated by different factors, or combinations of factors, and that this is also dependent on the circumstances.

The possibility of cheating

The possibility of abusing the system can occur in two ways, firstly when working through the cards, and secondly when taking a test: 'If they took the answers from the back, you'd have to work through the cards to answer the test. You wouldn't have any choice, because you wouldn't be able to work back from the answers then.' Many pupils said they are tempted, if they get stuck, just to copy down the answers rather than asking for assistance, particularly when working on a booklet, where the answers are 'glaring you in the face'. If the answers were to be removed, one pupil pointed out that 'it'd cause more problems, because every time you finished a card you'd have to go up and have it marked'.

An alternative would be for there to be separate answer booklets, which would make it less tempting, but still possible, to cheat. However, looking at the answers can be viewed more positively, since they may be used to assist understanding.

> If the teacher's got a load of people up there, and you don't know the answer, you can't work it out, you can always look at the answers yourself, and when you've got the answer in your mind, you could work out how they got the answer from the question; you could do it that way.

One pupil agreed that teachers try to check that pupils have mastered the material as cards are 'signed off', but thought that this is not foolproof: 'Yes, [the teacher] asks us a couple of questions, just picks out a couple of the hardest things, and if you don't know them, then just tells you how to do it.' However several pupils said that they do use the answers in a sensible way, without cheating.

There is mixed feeling about whether those who do cheat on the cards will be caught out by the tests. Some feel that this is the case. 'On the cards, because they've got the answers on the back, you think some people might cheat, but it's not worth it because of the test . . . you've got to do it properly, really, or else you'll have a really bad test.' But others are doubtful: 'The tests aren't really long enough. There's only about one or two questions, and you can go and get the card, and keep looking through the card . . . and you can usually get it.'

In other words it is possible to do the tests without working properly through the cards. It is clear that in many cases pupils do refer back to the cards during tests, and one or two said that their teacher would sometimes give them hints if they got really stuck. There is also the opportunity for actual cheating on tests in the form of copying answers from other pupils: 'You can ask everybody else if they've done the test, and they'll tell you the answers to it.' This is 'very difficult to stop unless you sit everybody in an individual room on their own, which there isn't really the room for'. It was thought by one pupil that cheating on tests might enable a dishonest candidate to get an artificially high CSE coursework grade.

It was not clear from the interviews to what extent abuse of the KMP system is practised, but it *was* clear that pupils realize that the possibility exists, that they believe cheating on tests does sometimes happen, and that this is regarded by some as a serious disadvantage of the KMP system, with it being possible to make apparent progress without genuine learning: 'It's a shame, I think, especially on tests.' 'That's a big downfall of KMP, that it's possible to just sort of slide your way through, the whole way.' However, the fact that several interviewed pupils stated that the tests do discourage cheating on the cards may indicate that cheating on the tests is not such a serious problem, and it was pointed out that not all pupils would be willing to tell others the answers if asked. However, misuse of answers on cards is thought by some pupils to be widespread.

Summary and Conclusions

Both case-study schools appear to provide favourable environments for the introduction and development of a curriculum project such as KMP. The operation of KMP is generally consistent with the aims and principles of the project, although details of its application in practice have been modified and refined over a period of evolution of 13 or 14 years. Both schools are of the 'high-school' type, with selective transfer at 13+, but there are significant differences in their use of the system. At school Y there is little variation between sets in the proportion of maths periods devoted to KMP, and this variation does not depend on pupil 'ability', whereas at school X a high proportion of periods are KMP for higher sets, while lower 4th- and 5th-year sets do no KMP. This reflects the firm belief at school X that KMP is less suitable (or not suitable) for mathematically weaker pupils. The upper schools have not adopted KMP, and this perhaps casts some doubt also on the suitability of the system for older pupils who are mathematically able. It is significant that in neither case-study school is KMP used for *all* maths periods by any set. The project is not, therefore, seen as providing for any pupils' entire mathematical needs, and interviewed teachers were unanimous that some traditionally taught lessons are desirable. These enable teachers to counteract any perceived weaknesses in the system. School Y also supplements the KMP materials with SMP booklets, and both schools have their own teaching syllabuses on which work in mathematics is based, linked to KMP levels. The CAL is used for internal assessment purposes, but both schools also set other tests.

Staff endorse the general principles of graded tests. They believe that pupils should be presented with work at an appropriate level of difficulty for them to have a good chance of success. It follows that tasks at one level should be mastered before pupils proceed to the next. The KMP testing structure is used to diagnose areas of weakness, and tasks may be repeated in order for success to be attained. The system provides clear, progressive targets and allows individuals to progress at their own rates. The two departments are committed to individualized learning in mathematics not only for its advantages in the acquisition of knowledge and skills, but also in terms of giving pupils greater responsibility for their own learning. However, careful monitoring and guidance are regarded as essential. Teachers expressed mixed views on the motivational effects of KMP. It was argued that the system can reinforce motivation for pupils who are well-motivated already, but that it does not necessarily create positive motivation, and can produce frustration for less able pupils.

Disadvantages of KMP seen by the teachers are that it requires a high level of resources, and it is open to abuse by pupils (slacking or cheating). There are also certain other reservations, for example doubts about continuity, and about its lack of emphasis on layout of work. KMP teaching is felt by staff to require good organization, in terms of record keeping, resource management and keeping up to date with marking. It can be tiring, but teachers in the case-study schools do not complain about the workload, which is seen as necessary and worth the effort in terms of results. Staff have built up considerable expertise in the efficient administration and successful operation of the system.

The pupils expressed a very wide range of views concerning KMP, although it is probable that junior boys and girls are more enthusiastic than the 4th-, 5th- and 6th-year pupils who were interviewed. This was the researcher's impression from lesson observation, and is also the view of teachers. The Head of Department Y felt that recent improvements in the way KMP is operated in the school are a factor in pupil enthusiasm, and that it was a pity that no 3rd-year pupils were interviewed. Overall, the interviewed pupils see fewer advantages in the KMP system compared with traditional methods than do their teachers. There were criticisms by some of the way mathematics is presented on the cards, and a number of pupils believe they learn better by listening to a teacher rather than by reading KMP materials. Some would prefer no KMP, but the mixture of both types of period is often liked, and some pupils think they learn better in KMP periods. The main perceived advantage of KMP is the opportunity to work at one's own pace, but many pupils pointed out the drawbacks that pupils are also given the opportunity to slack, and the possibility of cheating. There is considerable support for the KMP testing structure, and most pupils are happy for KMP levels to count towards external examination results. No clear pattern emerged on the issue of motivation; different factors (or a combination of factors) are important for different individuals.

KMP should perhaps be regarded first and foremost in terms of pedagogical reform. Individualized learning from workcards transforms traditional mathematics classroom practice, and the KMP system defines a clear structure of classroom activities for both teachers and pupils. It is only necessary for the teacher to announce at the beginning of a period that it is to be KMP; no further general instructions or explanations are needed for the lesson to proceed. KMP requires teachers to reconsider their professional role and to adjust to become a facilitator of learning rather than an expositor or instructor. These fundamental aspects of the system act in parallel with the features (level-progression, success-orientation, curriculum-linking of tests) which identify KMP as a graded test scheme.

Other Schemes in Mathematics

The Secondary Mathematics Individualized Learning Experiment (SMILE) is in many respects similar to KMP, and indeed was originally an offshoot of it, although it has become more innovative in the use of computers and in investigative work. It was established in 1972 within ILEA and there are eleven levels designed with ages 11–16 in mind.

> SMILE is a scheme for individualized learning, designed for use with mixed-ability classes, although it can be used with streamed classes as well. Efforts are made to provide tasks that are suited to each pupil's ability and experience. The emphasis is on the pupils learning from activities that they carry on independently, using the teacher as one resource among many, and not on formal teaching and teacher directed class activities (Secondary Mathematics Individualized Learning Experiment, 1980, quoted in Bardell, Fearnley and Fowles, 1984, p. 11).

One aspect of both KMP and SMILE uncommon among graded test schemes is that no certificates or descriptive statements of attainment are issued.

Graded Assessment in Mathematics (GAIM) is one of a number of graded assessment projects being developed in the London area as a result of collaboration between the University of London School Examinations Board, ILEA and King's College (KQC), which also includes projects in English, French, Urdu, CDT and science. In mathematics, GAIM aims to produce a complete scheme of graded assessment appropriate to the age range 13–16, and suitable across the ability range; it does possess the three key features identified in Chapter 1. The scheme is intended to be flexible enough to be usable by any mathematics department in any type of school (GAIM, 1983). The project team includes seconded teachers, and other teachers are involved in working groups and in pilot schools. There are four components:

> practical problem solving;
> investigations;
> extended pieces of work;
> content criteria.

Teaching materials are being produced to accompany assessment material, and GAIM may be regarded as an assessment-led curriculum development project, which in some respects draws upon experience in other developments in mathematics (for example, SMILE). The content criteria are classified by GAIM level and by topic area (logic, number, space, statistics, measurement) and it is intended to have about fifteen levels. The first pilot stage covers levels 1–3; gaps between levels will increase as the level increases, a common feature of graded test schemes.

The final two schemes to be considered in this section are funded by the DES as a result of proposals in the Cockcroft Report (DES, 1982). This report encapsulates much of what is currently regarded as 'best practice' in mathematics and in many respects supports the principles underlying the graded test movement. One of the report's recommendations is to establish graduated (i.e. graded) tests specifically designed for low attaining pupils aged 14–16 (the bottom 40 per cent). One of the two funded schemes is based at the NFER and is a feasibility study of criterion-referenced assessments in mathematics based on the Cockcroft Report Foundation List, and drawing on APU mathematics experience, in order to form graded tests. Assessment materials, including oral tasks and a circus of practical tasks, are being trialled in eight LEAs where there are liaison groups of teachers, and piloted in a further eleven LEAs (NFER, 1985). The project team is investigating how schools vary in the proportion of their pupils who fall in the bottom 40 per cent nationally. Another part of their work has been a review of existing practice in the assessment of low attainers in mathematics in secondary schools, which has identified fifty-one local schemes, fourteen of which incorporate tests at different levels of difficulty.

The other 'Cockcroft' scheme is known as SSCC, a partnership between the School Mathematics Project (SMP), Chelsea College (now amalgamated with King's College, London), two LEAs (Suffolk and Rotherham) and the Oxford and Cambridge School Examinations Board (representing COSSEC – the Cambridge, Oxford and Southern School Examinations Council). As with some of the other consortia developing graded assessment, channels of communication and administrative machinery tend to be both flexible and complex. While the fundamental aim of SSCC is to investigate the feasibility of a system of graded assessment following the recommendations of the Cockcroft Report, the scheme is nevertheless operational in the sense that certificates are being awarded (from 1984) to pupils in participating schools. There are two categories of these schools, pilot schools (using SSCC assessments together with SMP 11–16 Course G materials) and trial schools (using the assessments only). There are at present three 'stages' (levels) of assessment, involving written, mental, practical and oral assessment, with some opportunities for investigationary work (SSCC, 1984).

Chapter 4

Graded Tests in Science and Other Subjects

Music, Business Studies and Physical Education

There are established schemes in each of these three subjects. The *music* examinations of the Associated Board of the Royal Schools of Music (established 1889) are often quoted as a model for the development of the GOML tests, although there are major differences as well as similarities. There are eight grades of practical examination for a wide range of instruments, but for wind instruments and a few others grades 1 and 2 are omitted. Pass, merit and distinction classifications are available at each level.

> Each of the grades is designed to represent a defined standard of performance while the grades together form a progressive sequence of development in practical musicianship. The examination can be taken several times a year and the grades are not tied to particular ages, so that the scheme is tailored to the progress of each individual. Furthermore, as with sports, the choice of test items or pieces tends to be limited, with many elements, such as scales, known in advance (Nuttall and Goldstein, 1984, p. 10).

The Board also operates examinations in music theory, and in speech and drama, organized along similar lines. In 1982 there was a total of 466 284 candidates worldwide for the various examinations (Associated Board of the Royal Schools of Music, 1983). Within Britain and Ireland, there were 321 672 candidates of whom 90.5 per cent obtained a pass or better.

These music examinations are conducted on a national basis by external examiners appointed by the Board, which also determines syllabuses and sets standards. Hence there is not the element of teacher participation which characterizes the GOML movement. Another difference between music and modern language tests is that, in the former, learning and testing are individualized to an extent which permits easy application of the principle that candidates should be entered for examinations only when they are ready; it may be supposed that this is a major factor in the very high success rate mentioned above.

Turning to *Business Studies*, there are the typewriting and shorthand examinations of the Pitman Institute and the Royal Society of Arts. These are organized in progressive series of levels and the skills to be mastered by candidates are clearly specified. RSA exams are held four times a year and there is also a choice of entry dates for the Pitman exams so, as in the case of music, entry can be flexible and on an individual basis. The exams are set externally but marked in the schools. The tests are age-independent and criterion-referenced, with no possibility of examiner disagreement, and it would be difficult to cheat. There is no mark aggregation, it being necessary to attain the required standard on separate sections of the tests. Certificates state subject and level (in the case of keyboard skills, speed is stated), and are valuable for employment. A major difference with modern language schemes is that while these are school-focused, typewriting and shorthand are seen as being in the adult world; the Pitman and RSA examinations are not designed specifically with school pupils in mind.

In *Physical Education* a wide range of schemes are offered by national associations for athletics, football, swimming, gymnastics and basketball, often with commercial sponsorship. Some schemes may be more suited to club activities, or for school teams, than for use during lesson time, but this is dependent to some extent upon school policy. Schemes suitable for use during PE periods include the personal survival and life-saving awards of the Amateur Swimming Association.

No attempt has been made to ensure that the established graded test schemes mentioned in this book form an exhaustive list. There may be schemes in these (or other) school subjects which have not been encountered in the course of the research. In particular, there has been no attempt here to discuss schemes such as the Duke of Edinburgh's Award, which are designed for candidates of secondary-school age and are operated in many schools, but do not come within traditional subject boundaries, and fall more into the category of out-of-school activities than that of timetabled school periods.

The School Science Certificate

Together with mathematics and modern languages, science was one of the subjects selected for particular study in the research reported in this book.

Case studies were conducted in three schools operating the School Science Certificate, which has the distinction of being the first operational graded test scheme in science. This scheme originated in a suggestion at a meeting of Avon science teachers that something similar to graded tests in modern languages might be developed in science, a main aim being pupil motivation and the target group being 4th and 5th formers who would not be entered for public examinations. Schools were enthusiastic, Wiltshire joined Avon at an early stage, and other LEAs in the region are now involved.

Testing is entirely practical, and consists of a circus of stations, which may be tested in one session, or spread over several. Each station comprises apparatus, a pupil instruction and answer sheet, and information for teachers and technicians on how to set up the station, on supervision, and on marking. Equipment required for some stations is supplied by the scheme, and there is no cost to the schools for this, or for the certificates.

Items for level 1 were trialled in 1983/4 and this level has been in operation since September 1984, with 4 LEAs, 115 schools and about 7000 pupils then taking part. Silver certificates are awarded to pupils scoring 60–85 per cent, and Gold certificates for more than 85 per cent. A detailed list of the skills tested appears on the backs of these certificates (see Appendix 2). It is intended that these skills should form part of the normal science courses taken by the target group and that schools should not need to develop new courses as a result of participating in the scheme. Level 2 was trialled during 1984/5 to be ready for operation in 1985; it is not at present proposed to develop any further levels, but to make new sets of tests available each year.

The scheme originated in December 1982, and its development has been entirely due to the efforts of the working party which was established then. Progress has been very rapid.

> We took [the APU] practical skills assessment grid as our starting point . . . So the work of the APU has been quite fundamental to our thinking, but not in a philosophical sense . . .There's no good getting bogged down in theoretical arguments for this particular group of children. These are the forgotten tribe in most science departments . . . The more authorities that link into what we're doing, the more clout there is behind the idea. It's only of limited value in terms of employment; we're quite realistic about that. But the majority of children that went through the trials have never been awarded a certificate, or a pat on the head even, in their school . . . They were desperate for some evidence of success in something . . . The intention is to give these children some sense of satisfaction, something to work for . . . If it motivates the children to have some improved feeling towards Science, that's good, and if it

gives them a sense of success, that's good ... We think it's important, and it needs to be done, and it's not being done anywhere else, so let's get on with it (adviser, March 1984).

This adviser, who acted as convenor of the working party, felt that it would help pupil motivation to have rapid validation, and therefore certificates are issued three times a year. He emphasized the importance of success. 'What we're saying is that teachers must only put people in when they have a realistic chance of some sort of success, because we do not want children to keep on being told "You've failed again".'

The working party (which originally met about every three weeks) included representatives from industry and remedial specialists as well as science teachers and advisers (from Wiltshire and Avon). Individual members made up test items and then submitted them to the group for discussion which resulted in a set of stations to be trialled. The trialling process was felt to be very successful, and provided valuable feedback to the team as a result of which some stations were modified (or in one case abandoned). A working-party member thought that not everyone in the group was satisfied with the relatively low percentage mark required for a Silver certificate. However, he felt that the problem of where to fix the pass percentage had been overcome to some extent by the decision to have both Silver and Gold awards within level 1.

Although attendance at working party meetings during school time was a potential problem, schools have cooperated, and there do not appear to have been many real difficulties: 'You've got to strike a balance between inservice work and the needs of the children' (head).

All three working party representatives from the case-study schools had no doubts that the effort they had put into attending meetings and developing the scheme had been worth while, in terms both of achievement and professional development.

> I'd like to say everything that I've done with that thing seems to have been worthwhile. I don't feel I've wasted any time personally, let alone what these tests have produced ... I've learnt from other people, definitely ... You always felt as if something had been done, and you always felt as if you'd contributed something, and it was great ... One of the few times meetings seemed to be useful (working party member).

Schools wishing to join the scheme have been asked to send a representative to a local meeting at which an adviser has explained the operation of the scheme and the principles behind it. The in-service training is felt to be essential, and the scheme is seen as giving practice to schools in criterion-referenced assessment.

The cost of level 1 (materials, certificates) has been calculated at 50p per pupil, but there are substantial hidden costs, which are absorbed by the LEAs which are involved. LEA policy is to treat the scheme in the same way as CSE, and release of funds has been authorized on those grounds.

The three case-study schools were selected to provide as wide a range of information about the scheme as possible, within the constraints of the research. Taken together, they probably have a much greater than average proportion of pupils within the target group for the scheme, although this is not easy to quantify, and depends to some extent upon school policy as well as on pupil ability.

School S is a 13–19 mixed comprehensive with a mixed catchment area, school T is an urban 11–18 boys' comprehensive and school U is an inner-city 11–18 mixed comprehensive on two sites a mile apart.

Schools T and U are both EPA schools, and might be felt to provide a particularly stringent test of the effectiveness of the science certificate scheme. All three schools have been represented on the working party developing the scheme (in each case by a member of staff other than the head of science), and schools S and U were involved in level 1 trialling.

Use of the Scheme

There is a wide range of ways in which the certificate scheme might be related to the science curriculum. At one extreme the tests could simply be superimposed on an existing course, which otherwise continues as before. At the other extreme, the list of skills on the certificates, and the test situations, could be used as the basis for a new course. Neither of these extremes appears to be the intention of the working party, although the scheme is designed to be flexible to suit differing circumstances. Notes for the use of the scheme circulated to participating schools state that the tested skills 'may be acquired through use of existing teaching resource material', and the categories to be assessed 'would not represent the whole science learning programme for any course'. In between the extremes, the scheme may be used in a variety of ways:

(a) to ensure that the tested skills are included in the Science course offered to the target pupils;

(b) to provide feedback on the effectiveness of the curriculum in teaching these skills;

(c) to provide diagnostic information on individual pupils with a view to remediation.

A major aim of the scheme is to enhance pupil motivation by providing interesting, relevant tasks at a level of difficulty which, while challenging pupils, enables them to succeed and to experience genuine achievement.

In 1984/5 each case-study school used level 1 of the scheme with three or more groups of 4th- and 5th-year pupils on non-exam courses, group size being between 12 and 23. However there were variations in the way the scheme was operated. At school S there were no changes to the curriculum as a result of the introduction of the certificate scheme which was not given top priority. In fact the level 1 basic skills were already covered in their existing science course, and the tests were consistent with the course objectives. It was argued that the tests are linked to the syllabus not in factual content, but in terms of skills.

Pupils were not given any specific preparation for the science certificate tests, which were administered as a circus of stations in a single session under examination conditions (but in a normal timetabled double period), to the 5th formers before Christmas and to the 4th formers in the summer term. When the first group was tested, there was congestion at one station, and some pupils had to do this the following day; the problem was solved by duplicating that station for other groups. The few 5th formers who failed to obtain a certificate were given the opportunity to resit in February.* In their case information gained from the first sitting of the tests was used by the teacher to provide appropriate remedial assistance.

The head of science at school T believes that the science certificate should be taken as part of the normal course, and is opposed to the possibility of completely redesigning the course round the scheme. The three staff who have taught groups entered for the certificate have varied in the way they have administered the tests. Two have run them as a circus of stations towards the end of the autumn or spring term, but taking several sessions to complete the testing. One said that the certificate provides a good finishing point for his course, which concentrates on resource-based learning from various sources, some his own. His worksheets cover a range of activities (for example identification and classification, observation, experimentation, model-building) designed specifically for compensatory education groups. He feels that there is a danger that the science certificate might start to dominate the course, and encourage teaching towards the tests. The second is the deputy head, who is not a science specialist (although he has a science background). He had taken over a 5th form group after their former teacher had left. He felt that their previous science work had not been

---

*It is not permissible for a candidate obtaining a Silver award to resit for Gold; this is a rule made by the scheme in order to reduce the costs of administration and of the certificates themselves.

particularly geared to the skills tested in the scheme, but he had not needed much persuasion to try it, and thought that it had been a great success (out of fourteen in his group, ten achieved Gold and two Silver). Some of the skills (for example the measuring cylinder, the plug wiring) had been covered in their course, but others not (for example the microscope). He had permitted repetition of individual stations (unlike school S).

The third teacher had spread the tests over two terms, one or two stations at a time, and by doing it this way had linked the scheme more closely to his teaching.

> Some of the things on that Avon Certificate, I wouldn't have normally touched, but having worked on the scheme and set the thing up, on the working party, I found that this would fill a need in the school; it would make things a lot easier for me, a bit more structured, and would give a little bit of variation, and give them something at the end that they would not otherwise have. And so I've adjusted my teaching to fit in with that.

He had selected stations which were relevant to the work the class was doing at a particular time, and wherever possible had duplicated sets of apparatus to enable the whole group to be tested together. Towards Easter he had arranged for boys who hadn't completed the tests to fill in gaps, or to take stations again: 'Basically it was done in bits and pieces as the need arose.' His science course has been modified and focused as a result of the science certificate scheme, but remains much more widely based than the list of tested skills and includes, for example, sessions on car and motor-cycle engines.

The Compensatory Education department operates a Record of Individual Achievement which is 'an accumulation of neatly typed helpful comment on achievement' (deputy head) in class, in other school activities and outside school. The science certificate is seen as fitting in well with, and making a valuable contribution to, this Record, which is issued to all 5th formers in CE groups.

At school U about 150 pupils were entered for level 1 in 1984–5, considerably more than in either school S or school T, since the scheme has been extended to pupils taking the general science option, and to non-CSE entrants in a physics group, in addition to Compensatory Education groups. Asked about the influence of the scheme on the science course, the head of science said

> it has gone some way to hardening up our aims in that we see now the science course, certainly for the non-exam pupils, as being directed more to skills and processes, rather than hanging lots of

content and specific teaching themes to the course, so that given that we're using the Science Certificate as a backdrop ... within that, then, the teaching staff can explore whatever content and knowledge that they think is relevant and useful and appropriate for that type of pupil. As far as general science is concerned, I would have said that it hasn't really modified the curriculum at all in that we would assume that they would meet the skills encountered in the Avon Science Certificate at some point in the course anyway.

Most of the level 1 skills do in fact appear on the school's science syllabus for years 1–3.

In the case of Compensatory Education groups the course is flexible: 'I'm prepared to change horses in mid-stream if necessary, dependent on the response of the kids. It's not as if we were working to a set curriculum as such ' (teacher). He had introduced one or two things (for example the use of a microscope) to ensure that pupils could tackle the tests, but such preparation was very limited. In fact the tests can have a significant diagnostic role, with repetition of stations on an individual basis. All teachers involved with the scheme spread the testing out over a period of time, with pupils breaking off from normal lessons to be tested, a few stations at a time. It was found that the tests are easier to supervise if the number of pupils taking tests at one time is limited, with the remainder of the class doing other work. Progress has been monitored by recording scores on a grid of pupil names against stations. (Similar grids are also in use at school T.) The approach to the testing has been much more informal here than, say, at school S.

Test Administration

None of the case study schools has had any problems with the external administration of the scheme. Materials have arrived as required, and paperwork is limited to making an estimate of numbers to be entered during the year, and completing mark sheets to be submitted when pupils have taken the tests. Certificates are completed by a calligrapher employed by the Avon LEA (and are treated to prevent alteration). Schools may run the assessments at any time to suit themselves in the school year, but certificates are only issued at the end of each term, with deadlines for submission of marksheets. In some cases there has been a certain amount of pressure in schools to complete testing before a deadline, but this is not seen as unreasonable. Marking and monitoring pupil progress through the stations are quick and straightforward.

For internal administration of the scheme, there are several other factors to be considered. There is a considerable initial burden on the technicians and/or teachers to assemble and set up the stations. However once this is done, schools store the materials and equipment for each station in trays or boxes, and for subsequent administrations of the tests all that is needed is for teachers to request technicians to supply particular stations as required. 'It was organised very well, so that the whole circus could be wheeled out and wheeled back within minutes. So you'd just ask for what you wanted and out it would come . . . Never any problems' (teacher).

The number of duplicate stations required varies with particular stations, with the number of candidates in the school, and with the extent to which they are likely to need to repeat stations. Schools must ensure an adequate supply of consumables for certain stations, and make enough copies of the pupil worksheets.

Departments may have an agreed policy on test administration, or leave the decisions to individual staff. Issues are whether to impose formal test conditions or to administer the tests on a more informal basis, how many sessions to allow, whether all stations or only some are available in a particular session, and whether all or only some pupils in a group are being tested at a particular time. There are also questions about retakes, for example whether pupils may retake individual stations; if so, how many times and at what intervals; how much individual instruction to give. The case-study schools vary considerably on these issues, and policy depends to some extent on group size, on pupil ability, and on pupil discipline. For example,

> Basically it's rather a large class of very remedial children, which makes life very difficult, and the first approach I did was to try to do it as a standard set exam, and that was bedlam, so I cancelled that . . . I tried then to reduce the numbers who were actually doing it at any one time so I could keep more of an eye on them by giving the other kids different work, which entailed a bit more working on their own (teacher).

Several teachers said that supervision of the tests is hard work. A deputy head's view (after testing a group of only 9 pupils) was that

> it would be helpful to have a lab technician in the room when you're actually administering it. I feel that it perhaps needs two people. Certainly if you had 16 kids, I would feel that I would need the back-up support of a technician, simply to fill beakers, to tip stuff away and get it back to the beginning. Because when you're doing that, and putting ticks, and making sure you're putting the ticks for the right tolerances, your mind is actually being taken up

by a lot of other things, and I think it would be very easy to let something just slip by.

In the 1984–5 level 1 tests, six stations out of fourteen require the teacher to check each pupil's performance at the station, and seven need to be initialized for the next pupil. The teacher must at the same time exert discipline, answer pupil queries, perhaps direct them to different stations to avoid congestion and be vigilant for possible cheating, particularly if two pupils are working ₓt the same station simultaneously.

It was pointed out that teacher expertise would increase with greater familiarity with the testing procedure, and with the stations themselves, but that successful administration of the tests would remain dependent upon pupil cooperation. In general the view of the staff interviewed was that they could cope with running the tests with their groups, but that it was not easy.

The Concept of Mastery

In the notes for use circulated to participating schools, the scheme is presented as offering a criterion-referenced mode of assessment, and as providing a statement of mastery of skills. The level 1 criteria are listed on the back of the certificate (Appendix 2). Mastery levels are defined in terms of a percentage of the skills attained, and it is recognized that pupils may forget what they learn, by including the phrase 'at the time of assessment'. There is the problem of uncertainty about *which* 60 per cent or 85 per cent of the skills have been acquired. These percentages have been arrived at by consensus among members of the working party.* Pupils know in advance what marks are needed to gain Silver and Gold awards, and if testing is spread over several sessions they know how many more marks they need. In that case they may be able to upgrade a Silver performance to Gold by retaking certain stations (before their marks are submitted for the award of a certificate).

Teachers differ in whether they regard the Science Certificate tests as an integral part of the learning process. Some view the tests as separate from their teaching programme, while others take more of a mastery learning perspective, giving remedial assistance to pupils and enabling them to retake stations as many times as is necessary for them to succeed. 'That's the way I see it working, the mastery technique, and it doesn't matter how many times you repeat something, eventually if you master it, you've mastered it,

---

*There is the difficulty, common in graded test schemes, of reconciling the desires for both a high pass mark and a high pass rate.

even if it's only for that one lesson' (teacher). Those following this approach would impose a time delay, say of a week, between repeats. Whether or not the tests are used as a vehicle for teaching depends on the place of the scheme in the overall science course.

> I suppose if you tied the idea of the skills test as being if you like the backbone of the curriculum for the less able kid, then you would perhaps have a closer relationship between the tests and the actual teaching strategies involved in the classroom (head of science).

Another interesting issue is whether pupils must complete level 1 before going on to level 2. Pupils who fail to complete level 1 in one year may carry forward to the next year their marks on those stations which they have successfully taken. Although the tests are modified for each new school year, the stations are designed to assess precisely the same skill criteria. However some teachers thought that they would enter some pupils direct for level 2 and did not feel that it was necessary for them to demonstrate mastery of the level 1 skills first. A member of the working party said that many, but not all, of the level 1 skills are assumed in level 2. A holder of a level 2 certificate would not necessarily possess all level 1 skills. This appears to be an area which requires further consideration.

Technical Issues

In formulating criteria, it may be difficult to maintain a balance between the needs to be both precise and concise. Certainly, some skill descriptions (Appendix 2) are more precise than others. For example, Measurement Skill no. 2, 'Measure lengths under a metre to the nearest mm', may be compared with Recording Skill no. 2, 'Identify items of equipment'.

The skills are thought to be quite largely context-free: 'I think that they [the pupils] could meet a lot of them in a number of different parts of the curriculum; the measuring and the dial-reading and the graph interpretation and the filtering and so on' (head of science). However he was uncertain whether pupils would make the connection between what they were doing in science and what they were doing in other subjects (for example weighing in home economics, measuring in craft) or outside school. He argued that the tests are *content*-free in the sense that they do not require recall of knowledge. Another teacher felt that whether the assessment is context-free depends on the way in which it is used, and is related to whether tests are taken 'cold', that is, without specific preparation. He also thought that pupils are more likely to remember skills if the tests form an integral part of the course.

Apart from the context issue, there are some (minor) validity problems with the certificate descriptions. For example, it is not made clear that not all manipulative sub-skills are tested (for example, no bunsen burner was used in the 1984/5 tests). Another point is that several skills mention colour; however the notes for teachers state that colour-blind candidates may be assisted to complete the relevant stations. Candidates with reading difficulties may fail to understand the instructions, even though they are able to perform the skills.*

> You go up and have a look and they're doing something completely wrong because they haven't read the things in the proper order . . .
> They can read the words, but it's a matter of reading the sentences, and realizing that there are separate stages (teacher).

The ability to understand and carry out a sequence of instructions is not listed as a level 1 skill. This teacher suggested enlisting the help of the English department to teach the English required for following the instructions. That there are severe reading disabilities in the target group was illustrated by a 4th-form boy in an observed testing session. He was unable to read the word 'situation'; he could read the word 'hazard', but did not know its meaning.

There are also test-reliability problems. Firstly, there were twenty-seven listed skills but only thirty-three available marks in the 1984/5 level 1 tests (six skills being tested twice). The number of test items is dependent upon logistic and motivational, as well as reliability, considerations. Secondly, there is very considerable permissible variation in test conditions; it is unlikely that a particular candidate would reach the same score if the tests were administered (a) under formal conditions in a single session with no specific preparation, (b) under informal conditions over many sessions with the opportunity for remedial attention and re-takes. Thirdly, teacher judgment is needed in deciding what assistance to give to pupils who ask for help during a test.

> In my own mind, I was quite happy to interpret English for them if they asked, but I didn't wish to give them help in how to do something, or what they were doing, in other words in the skill we were trying to measure (deputy head).

He also felt that there were some items where marking might be subjective: 'I could see a situation arising where I might make a judgment which

---

*Again, the notes for use of the scheme do allow the instructions to be read out to candidates, but one teacher felt that one of the reasons for teaching science to these pupils is that it combines reading and writing skills with practical skills.

another teacher in another school might not make.'

Cheating is seen as a strong possibility: 'You've just got to try and keep your eyes open all the time, have eyes in the back of your head. With that sort of kid, they're going to try it on anyway' (teacher). It may be hard to draw a clear line between cheating and permissible assistance, particularly in classes where the teacher encourages a spirit of cooperation in normal teaching. In at least one group, pupils had worked in pairs on some stations.

It would be possible to overemphasize considerations of test reliability:

If a kid's able to wire a plug, and he's done it, then he's satisfied that criterion. Whether he did it along with a load of other stuff, or the next day after being shown, he's done it. What's the difference? (teacher)

This teacher, a working party representative, felt that teachers should be free to operate the scheme in the ways that they feel to be best. However, another teacher thought that 'it's not very fair from the testing point of view if I teach somebody how to do something, and then immediately test them on it'.

It is debatable as to how rigorous one should be in scrutinizing test conditions when a main aim is pupil motivation. If certificates are to be used by employers or selectors, validity and reliability of the tests could be argued to become more important. Equally, the more care taken the higher the status of the tests is likely to be in the eyes of the pupils themselves.

Status of the Certificates

It may be asked for whom the list of skills on the certificates is written. It would not seem to be designed for the pupils themselves since much of the language is inaccessible to the target group in terms of structure and vocabulary (for example manipulative, potentiometer). Another possible group of users is that of employers: 'I think it's useful for employers in the sense that they can at least see the kinds of skills that these children are capable of in terms of the science field' (head). He thought that employers are not yet aware of the scheme, but that dissemination would come through CBI schools/industry links. Several teachers felt that the certificates could be valuable as a component in a profile of achievement, and could provide a basis for conversation with an interviewer.

'If something is validated county-wide, then I think probably it's of more significance than a school doing a leavers' certificate ... because at least an employer knows there are some terms of reference or some criteria, so that the standard is equitable (deputy head).

Another teacher (a working party member) pointed out that credibility of the science certificates is dependent on teachers in the schools maintaining the standard, since there is no system of moderation. It is accepted that the scheme is unlikely to increase the number of available jobs, and that GCSE certificates would carry much more weight with employers. Nevertheless it was hoped that the science certificates would have some value: 'If they do help employers eventually to make a decision on the child, on the candidate for a job, then they're bound to be a good thing, I would have thought' (teacher).

However, not all agree: 'Employers, I wouldn't think, would take any notice of it' (head of science). He feels that the main benefits of the scheme are internal, in terms of diagnosis, curriculum feedback, and pupil motivation. There was no evidence either way as to whether pupils have actually used the certificates in job applications or interviews.

Another issue related to the status of the scheme arises from the target group being specifically 'non-exam' pupils.

> The danger of the science scheme I see is that since it is devised only for the less academic children, then it's going to have this kind of stigma on it, and the only way you can get over that, I think, is that you can operate it on the basis that there are certain skills that you must have in science, that all children should have, and there should be accreditation for all of them (head).

He favours establishing a number of levels, with more able pupils being able to bypass some levels, or only entering at higher levels. He felt that in some schools staff might attach less importance to the scheme if it is only aimed at the less able. Other comments concerned the status of the scheme in the eyes of the pupils.

> Those kids look at [the scheme], and they say to me 'But none of the other kids in the school are doing it. Why not?' And I have to say to them at the moment 'Well it's at a pilot stage. But there is every intention that we shall extend those levels.' Now as soon as they see it in the perspective of the whole school, or of other kids, other than them, that again gives it status as far as they're concerned. They think it's just something for 'thickies', and I was at great pains to point out that this was the beginning of something which we hoped would extend further. And they would be therefore part of a scheme for many, many other children of many abilities. And that's how it should be (deputy head).

He also felt that being observed and interviewed as part of the research had given his group an added sense of importance. However, another teacher played down the importance of the tests: 'You don't want to make too big a thing of it . . . Because the idea was that it wouldn't be an examination, and that you wouldn't put them off by making a great issue of it.'

Several interviewed teachers did *not* think the scheme should be extended further than level 2. One did not accept the stigma argument: 'An outsider would think that there would be a stigma attached to being in a compensatory education class. But it doesn't happen like that.' Another felt that it might be difficult to design higher level tests which were administratively feasible. A member of the working party saw nothing wrong with designing the scheme for a specific target group: 'What we're about . . . is giving them an exam to achieve well, and that's what this does for this particular level child'.

There was little consensus on the issue of the scheme's status (with pupils, teachers or employers); but it is clearly related to pupil motivation, which is the subject of the next section.

Pupil Motivation: Staff Opinion

There was general agreement that level 1, in its first year of operation, has had positive motivational effects on what may be a mixed group of pupils.

> Some in there have reading difficulty, some certainly have manipulative difficulty. Some are there because they have behavioural problems. Some are there because of attendance problems — irregular, infrequent. Others are there because they simply can't motivate themselves to work particularly hard even though they're quite bright (deputy head).

Several aspects of the scheme were thought to produce motivational benefits, which may be the result of a combination of factors. In all the case-study schools staff felt that pupils enjoyed the testing process, perhaps after initial doubts. Several reasons were suggested to explain the fact that the science certificate tests, unlike many other tests, were found enjoyable by pupils. One is that the overall level of difficulty is right for the target group; the tests are hard enough to present a challenge, but easy enough to permit success without appearing childish: 'Some of them have sailed through . . . Not very many; it's been a good spread. Some of them at the bottom have found it extremely difficult' (teacher).

Another is that the tests are practical, and provide a variety of interesting tasks which are seen as useful, and in many cases relevant to everyday life. The scheme offers short-term goals, and initial success gives encouragement: 'When they found that they were going well they wanted to carry on. When they found that they could do one or two then they became voracious for the rest' (teacher). Pupils do appear to enjoy performing the tasks required at the various stations, and this is irrespective of the particular style of test administration adopted by the school.

The achievement of success is seen as a significant motivating factor, and is particularly important in boosting the confidence of pupils taking the science certificate.

> 'They did derive pleasure from achievement, and I think some of them surprised themselves' (deputy head).

> 'These kids are so, dare I say, dim, that there is precious little they can achieve well in, and I think the thought of actually seeing something they could achieve well in, really spurred them on' (teacher).

Success in the scheme does not depend on competing with other pupils, and competition is not felt to be a factor.

There was a range of views on the place of the certificates themselves in motivating pupils. One opinion was that other aspects of the scheme are more important than the actual certificates, but others disagreed.

> 'I really think that these kids need something to take home, to be able to show that they can succeed at something, because the biggest difficulty is convincing their teachers they can succeed at something, but they've got an equal one, by the time they reach the ages of 14 or 15, convincing their parents that they can succeed at something' (head).

Several staff thought the design of the certificates mattered.

> They were very enthused, because the certificates are very attractive. They're well-presented, well-designed, and it has a wider currency than just (this) school . . . And that seemed to give them a modicum of self-respect over it. They felt quite pleased about it.

While no single motivating factor appears to be salient, equally it is not clear what the effects of the improved motivation are. 'I don't know if you'd say it is motivating within the rest of the science work that we do . . . I would find that difficult to judge' (head of science). He feels that social relationships within the group, and with the teacher, are probably a greater factor in motivating the class well than something like the science certificate. It might be that pupil enjoyment of the tests had improved attitudes, behaviour and pupil–teacher relationships, but he had not seen significant effects in terms of output of work, or improved performance. Other staff were not sure whether the scheme had improved the pupils' general attitude towards their science course: 'It's very difficult to make a judgment on that, because the course that we follow is quite an interesting one. It's a very relevant science course, and we get on well as a group anyway' (deputy head). A teacher from another school stressed that the scheme should be seen as *part* of the overall motivation of the course.

Some direct effects of the scheme were mentioned. For example, pupils were encouraged to be more careful with their work. 'When they found it was not accurate enough, or totally erroneous, and they had to go back and do it again, they started to be a bit tighter in their own performance' (deputy head). The head of a compensatory education department had found that pupils would now come and talk about doing the science certificate, who wouldn't have mentioned science to him any other way. He and others were doubtful whether the scheme would have any great effect on attendance, but some staff had noticed that certain pupils would make a point of being at school when testing was to take place, or that they would be prepared to stay after school to complete the tests. In one case there was a temporary negative effect on attendance!

> 'When they got their certificates, these quite hardened 5th formers — some of them consider themselves quite tough nuts — were in fact absent one day rather than receive their certificates in front of their peers . . . and in effect they had to be persuaded into so doing, but were secretly quite pleased' (deputy head).

It is possible that effects on any particular pupil are limited to the time he or she is actually involved with the scheme, and/or to a limited time before the tests are taken, and/or to a limited time afterwards (while they retain a feeling of success). Again, there may prove to be fewer motivational benefits when the scheme has been in operation for some years, although it was pointed out that each new pupil will come fresh into it. Interviewed staff in the case-study schools were unanimous that there have been motivational gains for less able pupils as a result of the introduction of the scheme.

> It's the first thing that's ever really been done for them. I can't think of a scheme that has taken off like this, that has motivated the very remedial kids, and actually given them something they can in fact aim at and achieve (teacher).

There have also been benefits for staff. Some have used the scheme to assist with structuring their science course, and all have had, at least in the short-term, better motivated pupils. A teacher pointed out that one positive effect of the scheme (and, incidentally, of this research) on staff is to make them think more deeply about what they are doing.

Pupil Opinion

Attitudes of pupils to the science certificate scheme were mostly favourable, with little adverse comment. The tests were variously described as 'all right', 'interesting', and 'quite fun', and pupils had enjoyed, or at any rate 'not minded', doing them, even if they didn't usually like tests: 'I didn't think it would be [a good idea] before Christmas, but once I got onto it, and working through it, I thought it was good to do' (5th year).

They prefer experimental, or other practical, science to written work or too much listening to the teacher, and the practical nature of the tests is a major factor in pupils accepting and liking them. The tests were thought to be fair, and the level of difficulty about right. Some pupils had found it rather too easy, but others had to repeat stations, having failed at the first attempt. Some who were interviewed well after they had completed the tests were unable to remember much detail about them. Of particular stations, those involving the tape-recorder and the microscope were frequently mentioned, and thought to be interesting and quite demanding, while station D (animals and paper-cutting) was often criticized as being particularly easy, and pointless. Some stations were liked because they were relevant to everyday life, or to possible employment: 'Doing that plug was useful, because some people don't know how to do plugs' (5th year). Two interviewed girls said that they, as well as boys, should be able to do these practical things.

There were some difficulties in understanding the instructions: 'Once I understood them, I could carry them out easy enough' (5th year). One boy who had taken the tests, but had failed to reach the standard for a certificate, said that he couldn't understand the instructions. He could read them, but he 'didn't know what you had to do'. Difficulties appear to be partly with the language used, and partly with dealing with a sequence of instructions, sometimes connected to what has gone before, and sometimes not. However, several pupils thought that they had lost marks because of careless mistakes, rather than inability to understand, or carry out, the instructions.

On the logistics of testing, the problem of waiting for a free station was mentioned, but was not thought to be serious, except perhaps towards the end of the testing. Some members of a group who had taken the tests in a single session thought they would have done better with more time. A girl (from a different group) complained about the behaviour of some of the boys in her class, and felt that 'hooligans' should not be allowed to do science. She also said that: 'There was too many in our classroom. Some had to sit down and carry on with science, and some of us had to go on with the test' (5th year).

There was a range of opinion as to how closely the content of the tests matched the science syllabus. The overall impression was that they had little specific preparation for the tests, and that many (but by no means all) of the tested skills had occurred at some stage in their science courses. Some pupils could not tell any difference between work for the scheme and their other work in science, but others thought it was quite different. One girl said that she thought the whole test was 'not proper science'. Proper science for her was 'chemistry, and things like that', in other words academic science as studied by examination classes.* In contrast, another pupil was definite that the scheme tested the right sort of things, although he also said: 'I hope the work will get a bit harder, because at the moment it's pretty simple' (4th year). Interestingly, he had not achieved the award of a certificate because he had been absent from school a great deal. Nevertheless 'I'd quite like to get a certificate to show that I'd done it all. Put it up on the wall . . . I'd like to frame it' (same boy).

Some said they were not particularly worried one way or the other about having the certificates. One had not liked receiving his certificate from the headmaster in assembly, because 'you just get shown up'. But generally the certificates were liked: 'I've never got an award for anything before' (5th year). This boy felt that the certificate proved he had done something; his family were pleased, and it is on a wall at home. There were many similar comments: 'I was quite amazed really, and my parents were quite proud of me, to have one . . . A certificate, you can remember your schooldays . . . what you've done in school' (5th year). She intended to keep her certificate to show her own children!

Some pupils might take their certificates along when applying for jobs: 'If you were going to work somewhere where you needed science, and they wanted some proof that you knew about it, you could show them that certificate' (4th year). However they were realistic on the limited value of these certificates: 'If you're going to take a job, the employers wouldn't know what it is. Probably never seen one before, would they?' (5th year). This boy said he would like a carpentry job. A girl who wanted to do hairdressing said that the certificate would be 'maybe a bit of help, but not a lot . . . If you showed that one to them, and another one came in with, say, O-level physics or biology, well they're bound to get the job straight away, because it's a higher grade' (5th year).

The certificates are seen as a motivating factor: 'If you work harder, you'll get the thing. So everybody's trying to get one. So it makes you work harder' (4th year). The tests had made them think, and some pupils said they had learnt quite a lot through doing them. One girl thought that

---

*There is the possibility (hinted at but not stated) that the tests are not 'proper' because they themselves succeed. If they can do it, it can't be any good! [cf. the discussion on pp. 100–1 on whether the scheme should be extended to more able pupils].

doing the scheme had increased her interest in science, and another that her behaviour had improved: 'I used to be naughty, remember? I used to be really bad . . . I started to be quiet . . . I reckon that scheme's got something to do with it' (5th year). But she thought that some of the persistent absentees in her class did not have much interest in the tests, or in science as a subject. A boy (in another group) said that he didn't think the scheme had made him work any harder, or enjoy science any more. But several others said that they *were* now working harder as a result of the scheme, although there was no sense of competition with their peers. 'It doesn't come in at all' (4th year).

A 5th-year boy who has a YTS place as a mechanic said that the science course and the Avon certificate had helped him to do things and to think about what he was doing. He was pleased that there had been no pressure from his teacher to take the tests.

The overall attitude of the interviewed pupils, towards the scheme was very positive. Many like science, and some thought that similar schemes might be successful in other subjects.

Summary and Conclusions

The School Science Certificate, in its first year of operation, has been taken up by a large number of schools in the four authorities concerned, and this in itself is a measure of its success. It appears to fill a need for some form of recognition of the achievements of pupils in the target group. The content, style and level of difficulty of the tests are all appropriate for this group, and the scheme has been well received by heads, science staff, and pupils, in the case-study schools.

> I thought it was a worthwhile venture. I think it is the way that certain things should be going in Science. There isn't a lot that measures, very often, acquired manipulative skills (deputy head).

> It's something which I feel very strongly is something we ought to do, and I'm delighted to be able to have the opportunity to do it. And as far as the kids are concerned, I see nothing but benefits and plusses (deputy head).*

The differing ways in which the scheme has been used in the three schools studied raises some interesting issues. First, there is the question of the

---

*These two deputy heads are from different schools, and have each taught a group involved in the scheme.

relationship of the scheme to the science curriculum. Schools, and individual teachers, vary in the extent to which the tests have influenced their science courses, and particularly in the extent to which the tests have been regarded as an integral part of the learning process. However in all cases the tested skills are seen as forming only part of the overall course, although they may form a specific component of the course structure.

The second issue, which is related to the first, concerns the procedure for administration of the tests. Dependent on circumstances in each school, this varies from formal to informal, and may be carried out in one session or spread over many. The number of stations, and the number of pupils, being tested at one time varies accordingly. Test supervision has not been found to be altogether easy, but teachers have been able to cope with a range of group sizes. The fourteen stations demonstrate considerable ingenuity, variety and applicability.

There are some technical problems of validity and reliability. The former are mainly concerned with the skill descriptions on the certificates and the latter are caused mainly by permissible variation in test conditions. How important these technical issues are is a question for further consideration; it may be paramount that the scheme retains flexibility for differing conditions in participating schools, or it may be desirable to introduce some moderation procedure.

Another issue is the extent to which the scheme is seen as a mastery learning programme. Relevant factors here are cut-off scores for the award of certificates, conditions (if any) for allowing candidates to repeat stations, and whether level 1 is regarded as a pre-requisite for level 2.

Various aims for the scheme emerge from the research, and their relative importance is perceived differently by different individuals and groups involved with the scheme. The aims are:

(1) to ensure that the listed basic skills are covered in science courses;

(2) to provide feedback information for teachers on pupil performance, which may be used for individual diagnosis and remediation, or for modification of the course;

(3) to contribute to the overall assessment system in the school (the scheme may form a component of a Mode 3 proposal, or be linked to a school profile of attainment);

(4) to provide a statement (for example for employers) of what science skills pupils have attained;

(5) to increase pupil motivation.

The certificates appear to have limited value in employment terms, but do provide tangible evidence of pupil achievement (for example, for parents). Perhaps the most important single aspect of the scheme is the opportunity it provides for pupils to experience success. In addition to the extrinsic motivation of the certificates, the tests themselves offer intrinsic motivation by giving pupils tasks which are enjoyable, interesting, relevant, and difficult enough to provide a challenge while sufficiently within pupils' grasp to give a realistic chance of success, thus allowing a genuine sense of achievement. Evidence that the scheme does have positive motivational benefits is given by the teachers and pupils interviewed in the course of the research. However it is not clear to what extent (if any) there is carry-over to the remainder of the science course, or to what extent motivational gains will continue after the scheme ceases to be novel. Effects on pupil attendance appear to be minimal (although positive), and it may be that the main gains will be in terms of improved attitudes, pupil–teacher relations and pupil self-respect.

An issue on which a range of views was expressed was whether the scheme should be extended to higher levels or to more able pupils. It was argued by some that it was designed specifically for the target group and should not be extended, but by others that in order to maintain status it would be necessary for the scheme to be perceived as suitable for a much wider ability range. However there might be practical difficulties which would inhibit any possible further extension.

One final point is that the scheme has a significant in-service role for teachers, particularly for members of the working party, but also for all teachers involved with operating the scheme in schools.

Although it would be wrong to pretend that the scheme has solved all problems, either within the scheme itself, or for the overall science programme for the target group, the overall impression from the research is that it is achieving many of its aims, and the return on the investment in the scheme by all those concerned is considerable, although at this stage it is difficult to quantify this in terms of measurable effects on pupils.

Centralized Developments

We conclude this chapter with discussion on some centralized graded assessment schemes which are under development. GAIM (Graded Assessment in Mathematics), referred to in Chapter 3, is one subject component of developments in London. The parallel Graded Assessment in Science Project (GASP) is working within a three-dimensional framework in general science: content, process-skills and explorations (ULSEB, 1985 a). The emphasis on process is consistent with the principles of the Assessment of Performance Unit Science team, which appear to be widely accepted as representing current 'best practice' in science. Before a graded assessment scheme can be developed it is necessary to arrive at a consensus on curricular objectives.

> A major problem . . . is to identify those 'domains' of content which are common across several science courses, and another is to design questions which assess 'mastery' rather than discriminate between students. In both of these problem areas, expertise is being slowly developed by the participating teachers (ULSEB, 1985 a, p. 5).

As with GAIM, GASP is interested in methods by which teachers can assess process-skills using defined criteria in the context of a normal lesson, and 'Investigations are being started into the number of times students have to be assessed before it can be reasonably assumed that they have achieved the competence level required' (ULSEB, 1985 a, p. 5).

Developments in the other subject areas are less advanced, but the inclusion of Urdu is worth comment. Broadbent and Mehta (1985) support the development of graded objectives schemes for community languages in the context of a pluralist society in Britain on the grounds that such development could 'become one of the major strategies whereby the status of Community Languages in secondary schools can perhaps be raised to that of the more commonly taught Modern Languages' (Broadbent and Mehta, 1985, p. 9). The notion that the status of a school course is dependent upon the underlying assessment system is not new, but it is interesting that the GOML movement is here thought to have advanced to the point at which it might confer prestige on languages falling under its umbrella. This is a possible function of graded tests which may be added to the list given in Chapter 1.

In English the London working group believes that progress is a developmental process of individual maturation, and that there are no well-defined stages applicable to all students (ULSEB, 1985 a). The team considers that there should be no overall levels (ULSEB, 1985 b), and therefore our key feature A (chapter 1) would require modification in the case of this English scheme. However, the scheme does possess key features B and C.

> We have pin-pointed some of the achievements that are accomplished by students and have described each achievement in the form of a statement which says something worthwhile about a student's work. A collection of these statements would form a profile of success . . . We want the scheme to reflect what really does go on in the best English classrooms (ULSEB, 1985 b, p. 1).

The statements are arranged in areas, and are not all independent, since some include or depend upon others. For example, the statement, 'The student can explain a sequential storyline' includes the statement 'The student can follow a sequential storyline.' It would presumably be theoretically possible for statements to be grouped in levels, although this might be a predominantly arbitrary classification, but this possibility appears to have been rejected by the London team.

A draft policy document issued by the Department of Education and Science (DES, 1983) expresses doubts about the feasibility of graded tests in English. Kimberley (1984) refers to the 'reluctance of English teachers to enter the graded test search' and argues that graded tests following the GOML model would be 'very limited and limiting', on the grounds that

> A test of communicative competence in a modern language after a number of terms of classroom study is a very different matter from the assessment of all-round attainment in a language which has been spoken with virtually full communicative competence from around the age of five (Kimberley, 1984, p. 23).

Although other graded test models are available, it may be that new forms of assessment in English will not be 'graded' in the sense of satisfying the condition to be level-progressive. Indeed, graded tests in English may not be consistent with a view of the nature of the subject based on the belief that individuals should be able to widen their understanding and use of the language along different routes, and that the provision of opportunities for appreciation and expression are as important as the teaching of specific skills (Pennycuick, 1985).

Developments in London have counterparts in Oxford, and in the Midlands. The Oxford Certificate of Educational Achievement (OCEA) is being developed as a result of cooperation between four LEAs (Oxfordshire, Leicestershire, Somerset and Coventry) and the University of Oxford (Department of Educational Studies and Delegacy of Local Examinations). Plans include subject-specific assessments in four subjects: mathematics, science, modern languages and English; there is a research and development group of seconded teachers in each subject, within a complex OCEA management structure. In the first OCEA Newsletter these subject assessments were described in terms of 'graded tests', 'graded objectives' and 'graded assessments'. A few months later, they were referred to as the OCEA 'G-component', but there were still references to 'levels' for all subjects except English (OCEA, 1983). However, later newsletters (OCEA, 1984 and 1985) contain no reference to graded assessment or to levels for any subject, and it is clear that there has been a significant shift in thinking within the OCEA group. As with English in London, our key features B and C are still satisfied, but not feature A. The reasons behind OCEA's move away from *graded* assessment appear to involve several factors:

(1) an increasing commitment to the definition of achievement by explicit criteria, without aggregation;

(2) the wish to avoid over-rigid prescription by artificial delineation of levels, and to maintain an element of flexibility in the ways in which school curricula may accommodate subject criteria;

(3) an increased emphasis on the P-component (student personal record), influenced by DES policy documents (DES, 1983 and 1984) which support the development of records of achievement while adopting a less positive attitude towards graded assessment, except in mathematics.

The recently initiated Midland Examining Group Project on Assessment of Graded Objectives (in association with several LEAs) is working on French, English, mathematics, science and CDT. The task of the groups of seconded teachers is to identify within each subject a series of performance criteria which can be grouped into criteria-related levels which will form the basis for the development of assessment techniques (MEG, undated). Thus it seems that the Midland Project will be more similar to developments in London than to OCEA. In all three projects there are significant differences in approach and emphasis between subject groups, which to a large extent work independently in developing schemes appropriate to their respective subjects. In modern languages (and to some extent in mathematics) groups are able to base their work on established graded test schemes, while in other subject areas development must be more *ab initio*. All three large-scale centralized projects are developing rapidly, but none is yet operational (October 1985), and evaluation of their feasibility and effects remains to be undertaken.

It is interesting that there appear to be no plans to extend the concept of graded assessment into the fields of the humanities or the visual (i.e. non-performing) arts. It may be that those working in these subject areas in secondary schools have not perceived a need for new forms of assessment, or that they feel level-progressive assessment to be in some way inappropriate for their subjects; the latter seems to be true in the case of English. In subject areas where the graded assessment concept *is* popular, evaluation questions for existing or currently developing schemes might include (among many others):

● Where has the initiative come from and what is the nature of the perceived need?

- What aspects of the scheme motivate the several interested groups, and to which functions of graded assessment do they attach the most importance?

- How is the scheme perceived by the participants, and what is its short- and long-term impact on teaching, learning and curricular organization?

- In those cases where the scheme is associated with curricular reform, what is the nature of that reform, and does it precede, or develop simultaneously with, the introduction of graded assessment?

Chapter 5

The Impact of Graded Tests on Teaching and Learning*

Graded Tests as a Vehicle for Curriculum Reform

Many graded test schemes may be placed in the category of assessment-led curriculum development projects. In each case a major curricular and/or pedagogical reform is associated with the assessment framework provided by the principles and structure of the graded tests. Whereas there is a common thread in that learning becomes more pupil-centred, the nature of the reform is dependent on the particular scheme. Thus in modern languages, syllabuses may be based on functions and notions related to authentic contexts rather than on grammar and syntax. There is much more oral and much less written work; the emphasis is on communication rather than translation. In the Kent Mathematics Project (KMP) the reform is primarily pedagogical; class teaching gives way to individualized learning based on a material bank of workcards, booklets and cassette tapes. In the School Science Certificate (SSC) the curriculum reform is perhaps less pronounced, but nevertheless entails a significant shift towards practical activity by the pupils themselves, as opposed to written work or listening to exposition by the teachers, and there is an increased emphasis on basic skills.

The key features of graded tests are conceptually separate from the curricular and pedagogical reforms associated with the schemes. An immediate question which arises is the extent to which implementation of the reforms depends upon the graded test framework. Could these, or similar, reforms have been introduced without such a framework? Would they have

---

*This chapter is a version of a paper which first appeared in H.D. Black and W.B. Dockrell (eds,1987) *New Developments in Educational Assessment*, BJEP Monograph no. 3, Edinburgh: Scottish Academic Press.

occurred in any case, given the pressures resulting from the almost universal movement to comprehensive secondary education and the raising of the school-leaving age to 16? Certainly some assessment system is needed, if only for reasons of status and for reporting pupil achievement.

The view adopted here is that these graded test schemes provide a convenient and appropriate vehicle for reform to take place. Several functions of the schemes support and consolidate the implementation of curricular change.

(a) They provide a learning structure which helps to define and stabilize the classroom situation for pupils and teachers. For example, given the single statement, 'We are doing KMP today' at the beginning of a lesson, pupils know what to do and what to expect during that lesson. Schemes can also act as a uniting influence on a department in terms of curriculum, pedagogy and staff relationships.

(b) They provide benchmarks of progress and a means of monitoring individual progress. This is particularly necessary for programmes in which it is not easy to monitor progress because they de-emphasize written work, or where learning is fully individualized.

(c) They provide comparison with what is done in other classes, schools or areas, and hence give status to the scheme in the eyes of parents, teachers and pupils.

It may also be argued that graded test schemes can hasten the dissemination of change.

Another interesting question is whether a graded test scheme could be developed, introduced and sustained *without* significant associated curriculum reform. Any new form of assessment is likely to have some curricular backwash effects, but it would presumably be possible to develop, for example, a progressive series of graded tests for a traditional grammar-based course in modern languages. However, this has not occurred, and it might be felt that incentives to develop schemes, and enthusiasm for the operation of schemes, stem at least as much from the prospect of influencing and reforming curriculum and pedagogy as from the graded test principles themselves. Curricular reform is more prominent than the assessment structure in perceptions of the schemes held by many teachers and pupils.

Graded test schemes can act not only as a vehicle for curricular and pedagogical change, but also as a catalyst to stimulate and facilitate such change, and as a lever to exert pressure for change. The graded tests provide a framework, in the form of a progressive series of levels, which is clear in terms of defining firstly the ground to be covered and/or the skills to be acquired, and secondly the standards to be achieved. Although schemes may be aimed at specific target groups the framework does *not* define the age of the pupils to be tested, or the time to be spent on a given level. There is often scope for flexibility in the ways in which schemes are used within a school, for example in deciding which pupils take which levels, in the order of treatment within a level and the structure of individual lessons, in the tasks assigned to individual pupils, and even in the way the testing is organized (although not all of these would necessarily apply to each scheme). Nevertheless, the content and processes to be assessed, and the methods of assessment, are usually defined with such detail and precision as to confirm that graded test schemes have considerable potential for curriculum control. However it may be noted that schemes rarely cover the whole curriculum in their respective subjects. Restrictions on the scope of the schemes limit the curricular backwash effects of the tests.

Curricular Issues

The progression of levels in graded test schemes may be compared with Gagné's (1968) concept of learning hierarchies. However, the allocation of content and skills to levels by the working parties which develop the schemes is often decided as much on a pragmatic and even arbitrary basis as by a logical analysis of which tasks are prerequisites for which other tasks. Horne (1983) distinguishes between 'causal hierarchies', in which success at a task is *dependent* on success at previous tasks, and 'likelihood hierarchies' in which success at a task is made more *likely* by success at previous tasks. He argues that likelihood hierarchies are not invariant, and that some pupils may respond better to a different order of treatment. Now graded test schemes based on individualized learning (such as KMP) do permit flexibility, and schemes based on class teaching do not prescribe, or even recommend, any order of treatment within a level, leaving this to be decided by school departments or individual teachers. Difficulties in sequencing material may be created by the need to integrate graded test syllabuses with textbook courses. Some schemes, particularly in modern languages, draw a distinction between testing syllabuses and teaching syllabuses.

Harding, Page and Rowell (1980, p. 3) state that the first principle of GOML schemes was that the traditional five-year course should be 'broken up into a set of shorter-term objectives, each one leading to the next and each one building directly on its predecessor'. But in some schemes it is common for pupils to bypass one or more levels, which leads to the question of whether a holder of a certificate at level *n* may be assumed to possess all lower level skills. This assumption may be dangerous.

A related issue is the extent to which pupils retain the acquired skills. Margaret Brown (1983, pp. 5–6) argues that

> for a meaningful graded structure it is necessary for the testing to be restricted to abilities which, once acquired, are relatively permanent. Thus recall of facts and rote-learned algorithms may not be very appropriate contents of a graded assessment if children are able to learn them for a test but liable to forget them rapidly later.

It might be that the probability of retention can be increased by appropriate choice of test content and teaching methods, with the tests forming an integral part of the course. However, the need for effective learning to include continual revision indicates that analysis of learning elements into a linear or branching hierarchy cannot be the only factor in establishing a successful teaching sequence.

Rote learning may be an endemic danger in an assessment system which clearly specifies the tasks to be performed by candidates (the 'curriculum-linking' feature). The more precise the specification, the more candidates will know what the test questions will be, and are able to practise accordingly. Factors encouraging teachers to 'teach to the test' in graded test schemes include not only precise specification of objectives, but also emphasis on success for the great majority of pupils (the 'success-orientation' feature). In some circumstances this might not matter if the specified skills (for example, learning to wire a plug) are in fact acquired. Indeed 'teaching to the test' is perhaps not very far from 'relating instruction and assessment closely to the objectives'. But it could still be argued that restriction of the curriculum to the test items themselves is undesirable. One reservation about GOML schemes in general is the possible use of testing syllabuses as teaching syllabuses. This might have consequent negative curricular backwash effects (e.g. excessive use of English), in addition to over-emphasis on testing. Some teachers doubt whether the schemes enable pupils to reach a point at which they begin to use language creatively, but over-emphasis on testing can be avoided by bypassing levels. In schemes where learning is individualized, again there is the danger of 'learning to the test', permitting apparent progress without genuine learning, and actual cheating on tests may also have this effect. Cheating may become a greater risk if different pupils take the same test at different times. But it would be a pity to overemphasize the possible negative effects of graded testing. There is evidence that schemes may be handled in such a way as to minimize such effects, and there are also significant positive backwash effects, for example, the achievement of greater stress on oral or practical work.

Diagnostic Functions of Graded Tests

The most basic diagnostic use that could be made of graded test results is guidance to pupils on whether or not to continue the subject. But in practice this choice is limited, since many subjects are compulsory, and options may only be available at the end of the 3rd year. Even then the decision is influenced by other factors: intended career, attitude to the subject, results in other subjects and timetabling constraints. Given that study of the subject *is* to be continued after taking a particular graded test level, then pupils who pass may be expected to proceed to the next level, or perhaps bypass one or more levels. If they fail, the situation is more complex. Pupils may possibly be expected to repeat the entire course for the failed level, although this appears to be uncommon. Alternatively, pupils may receive specific remedial instruction before retaking the same level, or even go on regardless to the next level. This last possibility may appear to negate sensible diagnostic use of the test results, but may be the only practicable option in a class-based scheme where teachers may feel that a class is only manageable if all its members are working at the same level.

In principle, pupils are not entered for graded tests until they are likely to succeed, but in practice pupils do sit tests and fail to reach the specified standard. This occurs sometimes through administrative convenience in entering whole classes for tests at the same time, but also because (unlike many mastery learning strategies) schemes do not place stress on formal methods of formative diagnostic assessment by which teachers may know when pupils are ready. Teachers might argue that such assessment may be done informally, but the point is that pupils do fail graded tests, and that diagnostic use may therefore be made of the graded test results themselves, even though this diagnostic function may be limited when the principle of readiness is in fact applied.

There are several points to be made. Firstly Black and Dockrell (1980, p. 12) state that 'diagnostic assessment requires clarity concerning the outcomes of learning intended by the teacher'. The curriculum-linking feature of graded tests ensures that assessment is indeed focused on intended learning outcomes. Clear specification of the knowledge and processes to be assessed assists the diagnostic function, and a wide range of test styles enables a broad spectrum of outcomes to be covered. Secondly, effective diagnostic assessment is essentially descriptive, not numerical. Teachers gain much more information on what pupils have and have not achieved from disaggregated graded test results, that is performance on separate items, than from overall scores. Thirdly, active participation by the pupils themselves may contribute to the process. For example, pupils practising in pairs on oral assignment checklists are not only diagnosing, but to some extent are also remediating, their own deficiencies.

Of course the diagnostic function is only effective if it provides both a process for detecting gaps and weaknesses in students' knowledge and skills *and* some mechanism by which such faults may be corrected: 'the overriding factor in all situations must be that the test should be positioned at a point in the teaching strategy when there will be time to do something about the problems diagnosed' (Black and Dockrell, 1980, p. 31). A drawback of many graded test schemes from this perspective is the tendency to set tests at the end of the academic year, thus leaving insufficient time available for remedial action. A further serious limitation may be in the time available for teachers to give individual attention. Schemes based on individualized learning are perhaps the most suited to the diagnostic function. Indeed Margaret Brown (1983, p. 7), in the context of mathematics, states that

> it would seem that the greater the integration between the curriculum and the assessment, to the point where the assessment tasks become identical with the curriculum itself, the more use can be made of the diagnostic benefits of graded testing in the classroom. However this has profound implications in terms of the organisation of the secondary school mathematics curriculum, and must logically lead to individualised or flexible small-group teaching.

She also argues that the more frequent the testing the greater the possibility of using the feedback diagnostically.

So far the diagnostic role of graded tests has been considered only as a provider of information for pupil guidance and the remediation of individual difficulties. These tests can also be used in a diagnostic way to provide feedback on curricular and pedagogical effectiveness, and on the quality of the tests themselves. Thus if it were found that students were consistently having difficulty with a particular graded test item, it would be possible to use that information in several ways at scheme level, such as:

(1) to modify or replace the item;

(2) to modify the syllabus content or skill tested by the item, or transfer it to a different level of the scheme.

At school level, teachers can use feedback information to modify the methods used for teaching a particular skill, or to devote more time to it. The use of a grid to record the performance of individual pupils on test items not only assists in monitoring progress, but also provides useful diagnostic information for the course as a whole.

The Concept of Ability, and Suitability across the Ability Range

Although we believe that it is not, the concept of ability is often referred to as if it were a measurable unidimensional pupil attribute. Its use in terms such as 'low-ability', 'mixed-ability' and 'ability range' (within a class or across an age cohort) can in many cases be related to the ways in which pupils are allocated to teaching groups. In practice, individual pupils' abilities are usually determined by their (norm-referenced) attainments, commonly measured by performance on tests and/or other forms of assessment. What is included in the assessment depends partly on which features of the curriculum teachers regard as important and assessable, but also on the content of text-book courses or external syllabuses. Where there is setting, account is taken of the possibility that abilities may vary from subject to subject, but for allocation purposes it is convenient to regard ability within a subject as unidimensional, although teachers do of course realize that pupils do not always perform equally well at all aspects of the subject, and may have abilities which are not covered by the assessment system used. Allowance can be made for variation in individual pupils' relative ability over time by building in mechanisms for reallocation.

Questions which arise are whether these norm-referenced concepts of ability and range of ability are appropriate in the context of graded test schemes, and whether some allocation systems are preferable to others for the operation of these schemes. Graded assessment is not designed to discriminate between pupils by measurement of individual differences, but the aim is for the great majority of those working on a given level to achieve mastery. In principle, provided the mastery level is reached, the actual test scores attained, and rank orders of candidates, are not important. But even if test scores are ignored it is still possible to use graded testing to define an ability range, by consideration of the levels reached and individual rates of progress from one level to the next. Within or across class groups, one possibility for differentiation between pupils at the same level is according to when they become ready to take the tests. 'More able' pupils may be defined as those who proceed faster and/or further through the levels, and it would therefore appear that the concept of ability range is still viable in the context of graded tests, even if it is no longer defined in terms of test scores.

If in practice the concept of (differentiated) ability is retained, that is not to say that the meaning of ability within a subject remains unchanged by the introduction of graded testing. Indeed the nature of ability is modified by the schemes in the sense that they assess different types of attainment than do more traditional approaches. For example, ability in writing may be replaced by an emphasis on oral ability or on practical ability. In some GOML schemes the multi-dimensional nature of ability is stressed by the requirement for separate standards to be achieved in reading, listening and speaking. In an individualized learning scheme, the ability to learn by listening to a teacher gives way to the ability to work independently and to learn from workcards. It may well be that individual children occupy different places on the 'ability range' as a result of these different emphases. Perhaps more significantly, many teachers regard the principles of graded testing to be consistent with a wish to play down individual differences in attainment between pupils. But there is no evidence that any significant changes in allocation systems have resulted from the introduction of graded tests.

A major policy issue for graded testing or graded assessment is whether to design schemes for a wide or limited ability range. The target group for the School Science Certificate is 4th and 5th formers who would not be entered for public examinations, and the Cockcroft Report (DES, 1982) recommends the development of limited ability 'graduated' tests in mathematics. Such schemes do provide an assessment system for less able pupils which goes beyond the individual school, but there is the serious problem of the status of the schemes in the minds not only of the pupils themselves, but also of teachers, parents and employers. However there may also be difficulties for less able pupils taking part in full-ability schemes, who may become disillusioned by lack of visible progress over a long time-span, by repetition of content, and by comparison with the achievements of more able pupils (Margaret Brown, 1983). Even if schemes enable weak pupils to experience initial success, maintaining this is not easy.

It is clearly difficult to design common curriculum and assessment materials which both provide a challenge to more able pupils and offer a realistic chance of success to less able pupils. One advantage of limited-range schemes is that they can achieve an appropriate level of difficulty for their target groups. However even limited-range schemes may be at a disadvantage for low-ability pupils in that they cannot cater for the possibility of a pupil doing more work at the *same* level of difficulty (thereby continuing to achieve success), rather than moving up the hierarchy of levels. Once tasks are defined in terms of levels, it may be difficult to convince pupils that progress is being made *unless* they move up the levels.

The desire to make a graded test scheme suitable for a wide range of pupils may limit its scope, leading to doubts about the scheme for the most able pupils. There may be concern about the transition to A-level courses, and there may be a need to supplement the scheme for pupils for whom it is not sufficiently stretching. The pressures of the public examination system and the need for graded tests to lead to some form of national certification has led to the development of Mode 2 or 3 examinations linked to some schemes, requiring certain compromises to be made on graded test principles, but enabling the schemes to be followed by able 4th- and 5th-year pupils. Perhaps a greater concern may exist for those pupils for whom even the lower levels of a scheme represent unrealistically high targets, particularly as they approach school-leaving age. However this is not a problem that is unique to graded test schemes, although some might argue that the structure of graded test levels may make it more difficult to overcome than would be the case in certain less structured systems developed in relation to pupil profiling for example.

Pupil Motivation

Many graded test schemes state enhanced pupil motivation as a main aim, and it is clear that motivation is a salient issue. Motivation will be taken to refer to goal-directed behaviour and 'positive motivation' to mean that pupils' goals include achievement of the graded objectives and that a substantial part of their action during appropriate periods is devoted to the pursuit of that goal.

A major reason for the introduction of graded test schemes is their intended emphasis on success. They are planned to avoid the drawback of traditional examinations whereby many pupils experience a sense of failure both by being compared unfavourably with others and by being presented with tasks which are of an inappropriate level of difficulty. Task difficulty may be defined in normative terms (how well others do) or in subjective terms of pupils' own expectancy of success. Nicholls (1984) argues that in the latter case challenging tasks are preferred — those in which pupils have moderate subjective probabilities of success. Graded tests are designed to provide a challenge while having a high pass rate, and success in the form of 'doing better than others' is replaced by success in 'acquiring skills' and 'passing tests'. As we have seen, this non-competitive form of assessment is not necessarily egalitarian, since some will progress faster and further than others.

It does seem necessary from motivational considerations that passing a graded test is seen to be synonymous with acquiring the tested skills, in other words that the success should be *valid*. Otherwise pupil perception of success may be short-lived. There is a tension in setting cut-off scores which give both a high pass mark and a high pass rate. Whether or not the scheme is certificated it is important for motivational reasons not only that pupils should regard themselves as successful, but also that they should be regarded as successful by others (e.g. teachers, peers, family). Success may be perceived during the tests (when pupils find they can do the tasks), or when pupils are told they have passed, or when certificates are presented, or when pupils receive praise (perhaps when they take certificates home). Motivation may be due partly to encouragement from past (actual) success, and partly to the stimulus of the prospect of future (hypothetical) success. Graded test schemes aim to provide frequent positive reinforcement of pupil motivation by means of short-term goals consisting of readily available targets. The idea that success and motivation can be mutually reinforcing is fundamental to graded assessment philosophy (see diagram). However the intended emphasis on success is not necessarily realized in practice, and it may be more difficult for graded test schemes to continue the enablement of pupil success than to provide the initial experience.

In the long term there is the question of what will happen if graded tests are extended to more levels and more subjects. Will low-achieving pupils still be well-motivated after they have received a number of graded test certificates, and have seen all their friends receiving them, perhaps many more than they have themselves obtained? Intrinsic motivational factors may be more significant than extrinsic factors such as certificates. However in all three case-study schemes pupils expressed support for the testing structures, and for the style, content and difficulty level of the tests, and this support extended to some pupils who said they do not normally like tests. The graded tests do act as an incentive for pupils, although older pupils feel that what really matter are public examinations. These act as a major motivating factor by giving national certification, which provides qualifications for further education and enhances employment prospects.

A further possible factor is extra commitment and enthusiasm on the part of teachers, particularly those who have been involved in the working parties developing the schemes, with an associated sense of purpose and of control over the development. If teacher enthusiasm is important in motivating pupils, large-scale schemes developed by examination boards might not necessarily be as successful as those developed locally by groups of teachers. A parallel point is made by Nuttall and Goldstein (1984) who suggest that the *graded* part of graded testing may be relatively insignificant, and that a modular scheme might serve as well. There is case study evidence that pupils are motivated by teachers who make the work interesting, but little to suggest that teacher enthusiasm as a pupil motivator is more important in the graded test context than it is in any other form of teaching.

It was suggested earlier that enthusiasm may be based more on associated curricular reforms than on graded test principles. If the particular syllabus objectives and teaching methods adopted by a scheme are predominant as a motivating factor, new graded test schemes might not necessarily be as successful as existing schemes, unless they are also founded on perceived curricular needs. A good example of such needs is given by the communicative approach to language learning. Pupils like the stress on

Achievement cycle

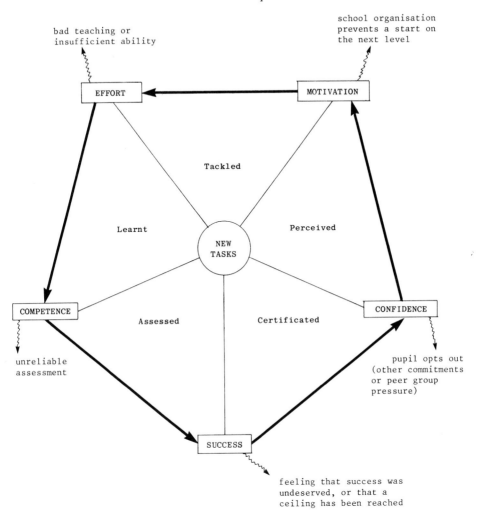

bad teaching or
insufficient ability

school organisation
prevents a start on
the next level

EFFORT

MOTIVATION

Tackled

Learnt

NEW
TASKS

Perceived

COMPETENCE

CONFIDENCE

Assessed

Certificated

unreliable
assessment

pupil opts out
(other commitments
or peer group
pressure)

SUCCESS

feeling that success was
undeserved, or that a
ceiling has been reached

~~~~→ denotes at each stage of the cycle
a possible reason for the next
stage not being reached.

authentic oral communication which they perceive to be practical, useful
and relevant. They enjoy the work partly because they can succeed, but also
because they regard the objective of realistic interaction with native speakers
to be a valid one. This extends to enjoyment of the actual testing process,
and can be reinforced by a genuine sense of achievement on using the

language, say on a day trip to France, although this is only a possibility in some areas. Clearly the style of assessment is important from a motivational point of view, as well as the curriculum content and the style of teaching. Another positive factor may be that assessment objectives are clearly defined so that pupils know more precisely what they are expected to do. But there are also negative effects. Pupils can become bored by over-emphasis on testing, particularly if the same topics arise in consecutive levels. Where testing is conducted on an individual basis, waiting for other pupils to be tested can create discipline problems in addition to the difficulty that no actual teaching can take place during that time.

There may also be demotivating factors in schemes where learning is individualized – loss of continuity, lack of perceived relevance, difficulty in understanding the workcards, or possible abuse of the system. In all schemes motivation may be a function of length of involvement with the scheme. In new schemes there may be Hawthorne or other initial effects, although established schemes are still novel to each succeeding age cohort of pupils.

A final possible factor to be considered is that of competition (or its absence). Many pupils do not see themselves as competing with their peers in the sense of striving to excel them, and would not wish to do so, but equally there is a strong desire not to be left behind. Pupils are motivated to keep up with their fellows, but competition is rather against targets and standards set by the scheme. Indeed graded tests seem appropriate for a classroom atmosphere in which competition among pupils is discouraged.

No clear picture emerges of what the key motivating factors are, or of the extent to which any improved motivation is a permanent effect. Different pupils are motivated by different factors and combinations of factors, and individuals may react differently in different contexts. The possible results of improved motivation, when it occurs, are that pupils will become more amenable as a result of improved attitudes created by enjoyment and/or satisfaction from achievement and/or perceived relevance of their graded test course. This may lead to several effects, notably better behaviour and greater effort, hopefully reflected in improved performance. Not all teachers are convinced of the disciplinary benefits. For example, an oral approach to language teaching can make lessons more difficult to control. Indeed it may be that discipline must in the first place be such as to permit operation of the scheme!

Nuttall and Goldstein (1984) point out the difficulty of analysing the key ingredients of the success of graded tests in motivating pupils. It appears that schemes can have positive motivational effects, which result from various complex interacting factors, with different pupils reacting in different ways. However, not only do these effects tend to decay with the time individual pupils have been involved with the scheme, but there may also be negative effects. Perhaps the conclusions for teachers are simply not to be overly sanguine about motivational benefits of graded test schemes, and to adopt a heuristic approach to their operation of the schemes with individual groups of pupils in order to maximize potential benefits, while remembering that there are reasons other than purely motivational ones for the development and use of graded tests, for example to provide a vehicle for curriculum reform, or to provide a clear description of pupil attainment.

Staff Perspectives

Graded test schemes permit flexibility in the ways in which they may be used by participating schools, and there are significant variations in practice. Department heads and subject teachers take account of several factors in determining the place of the graded test scheme within the course structure. These factors vary among schools and among schemes, but may include timetabling and setting considerations, resource constraints, and the pressures of external examinations. If the graded test scheme does not provide the entire course it is necessary to mesh work towards the scheme with other work in the subject, with topic selection and sequencing decisions being strongly influenced by the progression of levels. The 'ability' of the pupils and the logistics of testing are other factors affecting decisions about how each teaching group is involved with the scheme.

The temporal organization of schools, where timetable changes and automatic promotion occur at yearly intervals, does not provide a natural framework for graded testing, in which levels are not designed for a fixed time allocation, but where the intention is that pupils are entered for tests when they are ready. Even in individualized learning schemes there is a tendency to encourage pupils to achieve 'completion' in some sense by the end of the academic year. The principle of readiness is inhibited by the imposition of deadlines, whether the scheme is individualized or based on class teaching. In the latter case, teachers are likely to find it difficult to cope with groups working at different levels, or different stages of the same level. Vertical timetabling may provide at least a partial solution to problems created by the year-group structure of schools (the 'lock-step' system). However, mixed-age classes may only be operable on the basis of modular curricular organization, which again is likely to require fixed time slots, although if this were done on a termly basis it might become easier for pupils to transfer to a higher level group when ready, or to stay at the same level if not.

The logistics of test administration is a major concern. External administration (e.g. candidate entry, issue of certificates) is a concern for those running the scheme rather than teachers in the schools. It is the internal administration of the tests which creates difficulties for the latter. One is the increase in teacher workload resulting from individualized assessment. Application of the principle of readiness is another. A third problem is the time spent by teachers on testing as opposed to teaching, perhaps leading to boredom and/or reduced pupil progress. Fourthly there are disciplinary difficulties (e.g. preventing cheating, occupying the rest of the class during oral testing, controlling remedial groups taking practical science tests).

Several possible solutions to these difficulties may be considered. One is to conduct individual testing during lunchtimes, but this would increase workload still further, and does not appear to be realistic in the long term. Secondly, if resources were to become available, would be a reduction in group size or the provision of cover for teachers involved in testing. The availability of a second teacher would reduce or eliminate all the above difficulties, and some teachers feel that such cover would be the only fully satisfactory solution. Failing that, a third possibility is to reduce the volume of testing by simplifying procedures, reverting to a greater proportion of group assessment, or bypassing levels. It clearly helps if graded tests are seen as a *replacement* for existing school examinations and assessment procedures.

It is not only the logistics of testing which can create an overall increase in teacher workload. Teachers may find periods to be harder work and more exhausting than more traditional teaching. Extra work may be required to integrate scheme and textbook materials into a coherent course. Record keeping to monitor individual progress leads to an increased load. Workload effects on staff are cumulative, depending on the number of classes involved in the scheme. Teachers may be reluctant to extend a scheme to more groups, in order to restrict increased strain to tolerable levels.

The introduction of graded tests appears to require some increased resources in terms of accommodation and materials, and may also pose resource management problems. Teacher comment suggests that the availability of adequate resources is a significant factor in the viability of schemes. These include the provision of text-books and/or workcards, equipment and consumable materials, and satisfactory acoustics for oral work. Schemes are likely to be funded largely from existing budget allocations, both within the schools and within the LEAs concerned. It is clear that there are substantial hidden costs of LEA-based schemes which have to be absorbed. These may include major time commitments by advisory staff, secondment of teachers, costs of working party and in-service training meetings, secretarial costs and the costs of materials of various kinds (e.g. circulars, test materials, certificates). In general the benefits to the LEAs are non-quantifiable (e.g. pupil motivation, curriculum development, staff in-service training, prestige).

The need for in-service training is stressed by Newbould and Massey (1984) and by Harrison (1985), also by Rutherford (1979) writing in the wider context of criterion-referenced programmes.

> We have found that the problems with locally designed criterion-referenced curricula neither seem to be rooted in the basic concepts and approaches of such curricula, nor in the specific content of the materials which have been developed, rather the problem seems to lie in the fact that school-built programmes, and commercial programmes as well, do not develop a *support system* to accompany the content structure system (p. 48).

LEA advisers play a key role in such support systems for the case-study schemes. In-service support falls into three main categories, firstly written materials in the form of teachers' guides or circulars, secondly meetings, workshops or courses, and thirdly advisory visits to schools. It appears that the main need for further training felt by teachers is in the style of teaching and testing, not in the principles or administration of the scheme.

It may be supposed that the rewards accruing to individual teachers vary at least in part according to their depth of involvement, and their perceptions of the scheme. Harrison (1985) argues that 'the involvement of teachers in curriculum development improves morale and commitment'. This may extend to all participating teachers, but may be particularly valid for working party members, who are likely to have a strong sense of ownership of the scheme as a result of helping to devise the syllabuses and tests, and therefore a personal stake in its successful operation and dissemination. Teachers who have not been members of the working parties may nevertheless have sufficient commitment to the curriculum and assessment principles behind the scheme for this to compensate for any perceived loss of freedom to plan and develop their own courses, or they may welcome the graded test structure as an aid to curriculum planning.

Even if the scheme is found difficult to operate, staff may persevere since they see advantages for their pupils and perhaps for their own self-esteem. Increased workload is a potential but not necessarily an actual staff demotivator since teachers may feel that the scheme is worth the effort in terms of results. Staff morale and enthusiasm may be encouraged by a sense of satisfaction in pupil achievement even if teachers do not particularly enjoy the periods, and may experience a feeling of loss of control during them. A very positive factor is that graded test schemes appear to encourage unanimity of approach and hence departmental unity. Teachers who have adopted a scheme voluntarily are likely to emphasize its beneficial features in their own minds even if they also stress its problems to a researcher. There is the possibility that they may use the scheme as a means of obtaining more resources or recognition. Heads of department in particular may perceive a graded test scheme as a source of departmental prestige by drawing attention to their modernity and commitment, and even as an outlet for ambition. All teachers may experience a sense of pride from their developed expertise in the efficient administration and successful operation of the scheme. However, the overall impression from our case studies is that the over-riding reason for teacher support of graded test schemes is that they feel that these schemes benefit the pupils more than whatever they have replaced. It should be noted that many of the points made throughout this section may be true of any curriculum innovation, rather than being specific to graded tests.

Chapter 6

The Impact of Graded Tests on Pupil Assessment

Criterion-referencing

Criterion-referencing is often contrasted with norm-referencing, but this dichotomy is problematic, since criteria are determined by reference to norms. This is particularly true for graded assessment, where syllabus objectives, test items and pass marks are decided with the intention that they should be appropriate for the target group of pupils so that the great majority might experience success. Norms implicit in the minds of members of groups developing graded test schemes can be a major factor in determining the content of a progressive series of levels of increasing difficulty. As Houston (1983) points out, the notion of test difficulty itself has strong norm-referenced connotations.

However, once the syllabus, tests and pass criteria are decided for a particular graded-test level, then pupil performance is assessed in relation to the set standard determined by those criteria, not in relation to the performance of other pupils. This is consistent with notions of criterion-referenced, as opposed to norm-referenced, tests. Both graded and criterion-referenced assessment are designed to emphasize assessment functions other than discrimination.

A wide range of models for criterion-referenced assessment has been proposed. Some (for example, Gronlund, 1973; Popham, 1978) require precise conditions to be satisfied, including the specification of instructional objectives in behavioural terms. These models also require performance standards to be clearly specified, but it is not always a straightforward matter to do this. Specification of standards of performance in (say) athletics, or for objective written tests, is easier to achieve than in a field where judgment by an assessor is required, as in practical music examinations, or for oral language tests. In such cases standards may be difficult to verbalize, but exist nevertheless as implicit criteria in the minds of teachers and examiners, who utilize their experience, mediated by any training they have undergone. Such 'expertise-referencing' of standards is a feature of many graded test schemes. But however it is accomplished, specification of standards is dependent upon first defining the tasks to be performed, and designers of graded test schemes have a choice of possible methods of specifying syllabus and test content, with or without behavioural objectives.

Sally Brown (1981) defines criterion-referencing as follows:

> Criterion-referenced assessment provides information about the specific knowledge and abilities of pupils through their performances on various kinds of tasks that are interpretable in terms of what the pupils know or can do, without reference to the performance of others (Sally Brown, 1981, p. 14).

This makes no mention of behavioural objectives, and is phrased in sufficiently general terms to be suitable for inclusion in a definition of graded tests. If it were universally accepted we *could* regard graded tests as one form of criterion-referenced assessment. In that case it would be necessary to use a different label for the models developed by Popham (1978) and others; the term 'domain-referenced' is available and is coming into more common usage.

Mastery

There are several features in common between mastery learning programmes (as developed by Bloom and others in the United States) and British graded-test schemes. The most important is probably emphasis on student success; that is, on success for the great majority of pupils rather than for only a minority. There would be common ground in the view that motivation and success can be mutually reinforcing. In both systems the methods used to encourage success include:

(a)   a clear statement of objectives;
(b)   the sequencing of objectives;
(c)   the linking of tests closely to the objectives;
(d)   mastery at each stage required before starting to study the next.

Both mastery learning programmes and graded assessment schemes provide short-term goals for students, but most British schemes would not break down their objectives into units occupying as short a time span as the two weeks recommended by Bloom; one level of a graded test scheme might take up to a year, which is still short in comparison with public examination courses.

A problem is that of deciding on a cut-off score to separate 'masters' from 'non-masters'. It is clear that this must be a high score if mastery is to be associated with success, and if we wish to know with a high degree of precision what successful candidates can do. But one criterion in determining pass marks in graded tests must be acceptability to teachers and pupils, who are unlikely to favour very high cut-off points. Pilliner (1979) argues that 'the consequences of fixing too high a passing score may be boredom, loss of motivation and damage to self-concept in pupils who do not reach it', and another point is that the higher the pass mark the more precisely the tasks to be mastered must be specified, thus reducing course flexibility.

Bloom (1976) states that 'mastery is frequently defined as something approximating 80 to 85 per cent of the items on a criterion-referenced test', but the level defined as mastery in a graded-test scheme would not be regarded as satisfactory unless a large proportion of candidates do in fact succeed. In a GOML scheme which uses 'intelligibility to a sympathetic native speaker' as a criterion of success, it might be felt that a pass mark of about 60 per cent is appropriate, since pupils who can do that percentage of the specified tasks would 'get by' in relevant situations. Although there is a sense in which mastery levels are arbitrary, in practice they must not be either too high or too low. Graded-test pass marks are usually determined by the collective judgment of the members of the development committee. It is quite common for hurdles to be included in specified pass criteria. Thus in a GOML scheme with separate tests in speaking, listening and reading, candidates might be required to reach specified levels on each test as well as (or instead of) a given aggregate score.

The Principle of Readiness

If pupils are to experience success, they should not be entered for tests until they are ready for them. There are several possible strategies by which teachers can organize learning in order to implement this principle, bearing in mind the fact that, since pupils are likely to master material at different rates, it is difficult for the teacher to keep the class together, particularly in schools where there are mixed-ability classes with no form of setting or streaming.

Strategy A Provide extra remedial work for slower learners (probably outside the scheduled class periods) to enable them to keep up with faster members of the class.

Strategy B Let the class proceed at the pace of its slower members. Occupy the spare time of faster pupils, thus created, by either providing extra 'extension' work for them, or by using them to assist their weaker fellows. This strategy can perhaps be most successful when the graded test syllabus forms only part of the programme of instruction. For example, in a language course, faster students may learn formal grammar which is not included in the graded tests.

Strategy D Reorganize the allocation of school pupils to classes along radical lines (for example by the introduction of mixed-age rather than mixed-ability classes), so that there is sufficient flexibility within the time-table to enable a pupil who has succeeded at level n in a subject to move to a class preparing for level $n + 1$ at any time. It has often been assumed in Britain that age cohorts should progress through schools with automatic promotion from year to year, but an outsider might find the concept of mixed-ability classes far more strange than that of mixed-age classes. Such a major change to school organization might be difficult to implement because of complex timetabling problems, particularly if only some subjects were following graded assessment schemes. However, for a successful example of vertical timetabling in practice, see Pennycuick (1985).

Strategy E Design forms of assessment which are sufficiently skills-based to be virtually content-free, so that the tests become independent of the course material being taught. Teachers may then be able to introduce graded tests without significant revision of their existing class-based teaching programmes. This strategy has the support of several of those undertaking development work in graded assessment, for example in science.

Strategy F Teach a course to the class which covers all the objectives for levels 1, 2 and 3 (say), and then at the end of the year enter different children at different levels, so that the highest achieving pupils in the class will enter for level 3 without having taken the tests for the first two levels, while other members of the class will take the level 1 or level 2 tests. This strategy is possible in some GOML schemes, particularly if each level subsumes previous levels.

These strategies are concerned with the organization of learning. There are also issues related to test availability, and security and administration, if we wish to adhere to the principle of readiness. First of all there is the need to compromise to some extent on this principle if levels of graded-test schemes are identified with Mode 3 examinations. Secondly, Harrison (1982) explains that

> some schemes have test materials available at the beginning of the school year and schools ask for supplies of them (with reasonable notice) when required. This means that it is possible for pupils to take the set of tests for a given level at any time when they are ready, subject only to the organizational constraints imposed on the teacher. In practice, however, tests tend to be taken towards the end of the school year and in some schools are taken only as end-of-year examinations, by complete classes (Harrison, 1982, p. 8).

This practice is commented on by HMI (1983): 'while the original intention of a high pass-rate is achieved, the timing of testing is more often related to the age of the pupils than to their linguistic readiness' (p. 8).

The organizational constraints on teachers referred to by Harrison apply particularly in modern languages, where oral testing on an individual basis forms a significant part of the overall assessment. Unless teachers are prepared to conduct oral testing out of school hours, they may need to arrange cover from colleagues while they administer the test to individual pupils, which can be done most easily by testing large batches of pupils on the same day. Security may be a significant problem if tests are available to be taken by individuals, or small groups of pupils, at any time during the year. Parallel forms of tests could be helpful here, but locally based graded-test schemes do not usually have the resources to produce large numbers of test items of high quality. Considerations such as these may be important in deciding which teaching strategy to adopt.

The use of class teaching methods without some means of ensuring that the rates of progress of all class members are reasonably equal is likely to mean that the class will not be ready to take tests at the same time. Harrison (1982) suggests that 'the principle of testing when the pupil is ready can be fulfilled only when the assessment is incorporated in a planned learning sequence, which is not the case in most GOML schemes' (p. 19).

Schemes based on individualized learning can include assessment as an integral part of the learning process. For example in KMP, each pupil works on a matrix of workcards which have been designed for him or her on an individual basis by the teacher. Having completed the matrix at his (her) own speed he (she) takes a test on that matrix. In this case 'readiness' means 'completion of the matrix', and does not necessarily mean that the pupil has mastered the material on the workcards. As well as defining the pupil's level, the test result is used diagnostically by the teacher, who might require the pupil to revise some cards before going on to a new matrix. Of course if we understand 'readiness' to mean 'a high probability of success', and 'success' to imply 'mastery' in some sense, it is necessary to be clear what we mean by this last term.

One important issue concerned with readiness that we have not yet considered is the question of how pupils (or their teachers) know that they are 'ready' for a test (i.e. likely to achieve mastery), without the tests actually being administered. There are various ways of answering this question.

(a) Administer a previous year's test, as is done, for example, in 'mock' exams.

(b) Ask pupils to keep a checklist of the objectives to be tested (or of the tasks forming the test components), and to tick off each item on the list as they acquire the relevant knowledge or skill to their satisfaction (or to the satisfaction of their teacher).

(c) If an individualized learning system based on a matrix of workcards is being used (as in KMP), completion of the matrix might signal readiness. As already pointed out, this does not guarantee mastery, but is probably a better criterion than 'completion of the course' in ordinary class teaching.

(d) Experienced teachers can use their knowledge of the standard required, and of how the pupil has performed during the course, to decide when the pupil is ready for the test.

It could be argued that this emphasis on readiness is unnecessary, and that Harrison's (1982) assumption that the principle of readiness is a tenet of mastery learning is false. Certainly mastery learning programmes could be operated in such a way that a large proportion of pupils would fail to achieve unit mastery at first, and only succeed at the second or third attempt, after further study of the material. However it does seem desirable in graded assessment schemes, which test less frequently than do mastery learning programmes, to ensure that as far as possible most pupils pass summative tests at the first attempt. Repetition on a large scale would be unsatisfactory for administrative reasons and for motivational reasons in an assessment system designed to emphasize success. There might also be the problem of how to teach a class half of whom have passed tests at a given level and half of whom have not. If we wish most pupils to pass tests at the first attempt, then it does seem necessary to consider the question of readiness. However it might be the case that this is less important than care in designing the course. It might be felt that the main factors affecting student success are the choice of objectives, the structuring of objectives into a hierarchical sequence, the quality of the teaching materials and of the teaching itself, and finally the validity and reliability of the tests. Individual schemes may vary in the relative importance attached to these factors.

Mastery in the Case-study Schemes

In the background of all three case study schemes are the principles that:

(a) assessment is designed to determine whether or not mastery has been attained;

(b) pupils should only be entered for tests when they are likely to succeed;

(c) candidates should master one level before moving on to the next.

However, application of these principles is not straightforward, and may not always be achieved in practice. Although the schemes may be viewed in terms of mastery learning, this is not necessarily prominent in the minds of teachers.

The concept of mastery in GOALS is related to communication with a sympathetic native speaker and survival in specified situations (simulated in the GOALS tests), but this concept is translated into pass marks for the award of certificates, with hurdles at levels 1 and 2 in the three tested macro-skills of speaking, listening and reading. Specified pass marks are relatively low in mastery terms (50–60 per cent), since the tension between the conflicting requirements of demonstrating mastery and emphasizing success leads to a problem in reconciling desires for both a high pass mark and a high pass rate. The general view in the case-study schools is that cut-off scores have been set at a reasonable level. There are some doubts about whether all successful candidates have genuinely attained mastery, in view of the acknowledged danger of parroting, and about pupil retention of acquired skills.

In SSC, mastery is conceptualized in terms of the performance of certain basic practical skills which are applicable in a variety of environments (home, work or school). For the purpose of testing, contexts may be simulated in the laboratory, or the tested skills may be isolated from possible contexts. Mastery levels are defined in terms of a percentage of the skills in which proficiency has been demonstrated at the time of assessment. The problem of where to fix the pass mark has been resolved to some extent by the decision to have *two* mastery levels (Silver and Gold).

KMP tests are of a more traditional paper-and-pencil style, and cover knowledge of facts, understanding of concepts and performance of techniques. In this scheme, since no certificates are issued, it has not been found necessary for the scheme or for individual schools to specify *any* particular 'pass' marks, in terms either of separate tasks, or of the matrix tests as a whole. It is the responsibility of teachers to decide what scores constitute mastery, and to attach their own meanings to individual test results in terms of action to be taken, or even to negotiate this with pupils. Marks may be interpreted flexibly according to circumstances, and two pupils who obtain the same score on the same matrix might not necessarily be treated in the same way. In KMP, 'mastery' implies satisfaction in the minds of the pupil and the teacher concerning both the pupil's success on the completed matrix and the pupil's readiness to move on to a matrix at a higher level.

Thus mastery is defined (or left undefined) in different ways in each case-study scheme according to the features of the particular scheme and the intention of its development committee. In the two schemes where percentage mastery scores have been specified, it appears that decisions on where to place the cut-off point are based partly on criteria which include acceptability to teachers and the desire to achieve a high level of pupil success as well as credibility in mastery terms; the cut-off score is also to some extent arbitrary.

However mastery is defined, motivational considerations require schemes to be organized in such a way that mastery is attained by the great majority of pupils, and indeed success-orientation has been identified as a key feature of graded tests. Now if pupils are entered for tests before they are ready, schemes can actually reinforce failure. Organizational considerations may make it necessary to compromise to some extent on the principle of readiness, but it appears to be fundamental to the graded test concept for it to be preserved as far as possible. Of the possible strategies for implementing this principle considered above (p. 132) the most suitable for GOALS appears to be strategy B (extension work for faster pupils). For KMP the appropriate approach is strategy C (individualized learning) and for SSC it is strategy E (virtually content-free assessment). Some pupils in all three schemes do take tests without achieving mastery, but it is in the GOALS scheme where it appears to be most difficult to apply the principle of individual readiness, because of practical considerations and constraints due to the logistics of testing and the class-based nature of the teaching, which make it convenient to conduct much of the testing for the whole class, towards the end of the school year. It may be hypothesized that if this scheme is to achieve optimum motivational benefits, some method must be found of implementing more fully the principle of readiness. Rutherford (1979) makes it clear that the problem is a common one for criterion-referenced programmes based on class teaching.

Where there *is* failure, mastery learning relies on the provision of opportunities to re-take tests. Again, this seems to be easier to organize in the KMP and SSC schemes, where testing is individualized, than in GOALS. Failure may be only partial, and all three schemes permit success on individual components to be carried forward (subject to certain restrictions). Thus in GOALS, repetition may be of one or more macro-skills, in KMP of one or more cards on a matrix, and in SSC of one or more stations. SSC has the particular feature that if testing is spread over several sessions pupils may be able to upgrade a Silver performance to Gold by re-taking certain stations. In all the schemes, the achievement of mastery after initial failure depends on appropriate remedial assistance followed by the opportunity to re-take tests. In turn, this depends on teacher attitudes (i.e. the extent to which they adopt a mastery perspective) as well as on logistic considerations.

A final issue is the extent to which a level is regarded as a prerequisite for the next. The mastery learning principle that students should master current tasks before moving on to new material is applied most clearly in the two KMP case-study schools. Teachers argued that consolidation of the ground covered is essential, and mentioned the danger that children might otherwise push ahead too rapidly. The potential for abuse of the system makes it difficult to be certain that genuine mastery has been achieved in all cases. In SSC mastery of all the level 1 objectives may not be essential to success at level 2, and some teachers thought they might enter some pupils direct for level 2. In GOALS it is common for pupils to bypass one or more levels, for a variety of reasons. Teachers may not wish to over-emphasize testing, or may find the volume of testing imposes an excessive workload. A teacher inheriting a new class may find that its members have a very mixed GOALS history in terms of levels taken and certificates awarded, but will almost invariably teach a common course irrespective of pupils' previous GOALS experience. Nevertheless each GOALS level does appear to subsume previous levels, and it was pointed out in Chapter 5 that bypassing the actual tests does not mean that mastery of that level has not been attained. Even though graded-test schemes consist of a progressive series of levels, pupils need not necessarily be entered for the tests at each level in strict sequence. In some cases, pupils may even succeed at higher levels having failed at a lower level.

It appears that graded-test schemes (and departments operating them) adopt a flexible and pragmatic approach to the concepts and principles of mastery learning. It may be suggested that this is not necessarily to their operational disadvantage, but also that it forms a salient area for continual re-evaluation.

Certificates: Their Validity and Use

Of the case-study schemes, KMP does not provide a description of the knowledge, comprehension or skills attained by individual pupils except in the generalized form of a corrected attainment level, which conveys little specific information. Certificates are not, therefore, fundamental to the operation of a graded test scheme. However the other two schemes do issue certificates at each level which attempt to describe in detail what it is that successful candidates can do. There are several problems inherent in such certificate descriptions. One is that no guarantee can be given as to the extent to which mastery is retained. Secondly, at higher levels, it is not clear where a certificate holder may also be assumed to be a master of all preceding levels.

Thirdly, many graded test schemes base their performance standards on some form of aggregate score, and this leads to loss of information concerning individual performance on the tests, since cut-off scores are almost always below 100 per cent. Unless a checklist form of scoring (as in the driving test) is employed, and reporting is in the form of a profile, there are likely to be skills listed on the certificates awarded to successful candidates which have not in fact been attained.

In practice most candidates may score far more than the minimum required level, but there is no way of indicating this on the certificate, and for a pupil who has only scraped through there is no way of telling whether some skills have been well performed in the test and others not at all, or whether all skills have been performed in a mediocre way. But it may be pointed out that whatever the problems of graded-test certificate descriptions they do represent an advance on public examinations in which results are presented merely as a single grade, in terms of providing users with information that is both meaningful and manageable.

The tension between the simultaneous requirements for descriptions to be both precise and concise creates a further problem, of the level of specificity required in individual skill descriptions. There may be a lack of clarity in what is meant by a particular description in terms of difficulty, assumed knowledge or context. The same skill listed in two schemes may in practice mean two quite different things. 'The difficulty with such out-of-context descriptions is that they are too poorly defined to ensure comparability, and the more precisely defined they become the more rooted in a context they become' (Nuttall and Goldstein, 1984, p. 6). If a skill *is* precisely defined on a certificate, and thus rooted in a context, there may be little room for manoeuvre in designing test items, and such precision might merely intensify the 'teaching to the test' syndrome.

The context-free issue and other validity problems are discussed further by Murphy and Pennycuick (1986) but do not so far appear to have been major topics for debate within the GOALS or SSC schemes. Indeed there was relatively little comment about the certificate descriptions by either pupils or staff during the case studies, although any comment did favour the principle of providing such descriptions. The tests themselves, being the product of working parties of practising teachers, were generally felt to be fair and valid, although not all GOALS teachers were convinced that successful pupils have necessarily acquired the skills listed on the back of the certificates. Whether the wording of certificate descriptions should perhaps be of greater concern is related to another issue, the use that is actually made of graded test certificates by pupils and others, and this will now be considered.

One major certificate function perceived by teachers and pupils is motivational (see pp. 121–25). The skill descriptions on the reverse side of certificates may have some role in enhancing the status of these certificates by providing evidence that holders have acquired genuine and worthwhile skills, and that a serious process of assessment has been carried out before certificates are awarded. However it might be felt that the statement of achievement on the front of the certificates, and particularly the appearance of county crests and signatures of directors of education, are more significant for status and hence motivation than are the detailed descriptions of skills attained. Certainly if pupils display certificates at home it will be the front sides that are on show. These demonstrate that the schemes have wider currency than the pupils' own schools, and are endorsed by one or more LEA; they provide documentary evidence of individual success for the eyes of family and friends.

The identity of the main intended audiences for the skill descriptions is not clear. There is evidence from the case studies that some of the language used is inappropriate if many pupils are to comprehend it, or to relate it to what they did in order to obtain their certificates. For example: 'to initiate and maintain a straightforward conversational exchange, and to process related spoken or printed material' (GOALS level 3). On the School Science Certificate, several words (for example 'manipulative') are beyond the vocabulary of the target group. The language would perhaps be less daunting for pupils if teachers were to introduce it at an early stage of the course leading to a particular level and to discuss it with the pupils. This does not appear to be a common practice in the case study schools, but could perform a valuable function in identifying and clarifying for pupils what is expected of them if they are to achieve success. It may be noted that, in GOALS, the oral assignment checklists do act in this way. For teachers, the lists of skills (as separate from the certificates) not only perform the function of defining objectives, but also may be used to assist in the formative assessment processes of monitoring pupil progress and diagnosis of individual difficulties.

A further possible function of graded-test certificates is to provide employers or selectors with accurate information on what holders can do, and it is perhaps here that validity problems become most significant. However there is little evidence from the case studies that this potential function is utilized to any significant extent. Employers are used to dealing with national examination results which do not include descriptions of skills acquired, and although employers may in principle favour a move in that direction, some interviewed teachers felt that it would be necessary to make them more aware of graded-test schemes and convince them of the value of the associated certificates. Perhaps for skill descriptions to be of real value in employment terms it would also be necessary for employers to re-assess what skills they require their employees to possess. In any case the issue of graded test certificates (or any other change in the school assessment system) is unlikely to create jobs — the most that could be achieved would be a redistribution in the allocation of jobs. It might be dangerous to claim to pupils without supporting evidence that the possession of a certificate would enhance their employment prospects, although one area in which this does seem to be valid is business studies.

It appears that few difficulties are created by the validity problems of graded-test certificate descriptions, in view of the limited current use of such certificates. However if the situation were to change so that job (or further education) selection became more reliant on specifications of acquired skills, and less dependent on norm-referenced measures of attainment, it might be necessary to pay greater attention to issues such as the definition, transferability and retention of skills. Conversely, if substantial progress could be made on the resolution of validity problems, this might stimulate greater use of specific descriptions of pupils' achievements!

Test Reliability Issues

During the research, an interviewee argued that reliability is less important than classroom effectiveness.

> In the sorts of informal situations which the graded objective schemes have grown up in, reliability doesn't matter two hoots. What matters is face validity and face reliability, whether the customers are convinced that what is happening is worthwhile ...

Technical reliability is only of importance if those results are going to be used for some selection process later.

He expressed the view that the requirements of technical reliability have tended to distort test instruments and thereby to distort the education beyond them, and felt that a different concept of reliability is needed.

The 'internal consistency' conceptualization of test reliability appears to be inappropriate for graded tests on the grounds that (a) they are multi-dimensional and do not 'measure' a latent trait, (b) they are not designed to produce variance in scores by discriminating between candidates. Indeed it may be unnecessary to consider reliability in numerical terms, that is to devise a 'coefficient of reliability'; it may be noted that it is usual to discuss the parallel concept of validity from a qualitative viewpoint. Two aspects of reliability which arose from the case studies will be considered here. They are consistency of marking and consistency of the conditions of test administration, both of which may be conceptualized in terms of 'fairness', that is whether candidates have equal opportunities to gain marks. Nuttall and Goldstein (1984) refer to both aspects and suggest that, in graded-test schemes,

> achieving agreement about the criteria for marking among all those involved might be simpler than it is within traditional public examinations, but the variation in the conditions under which the tests are given and the variation in the tasks from school to school, and occasion to occasion, may wipe out any enhanced reliability of marking (Nuttall and Goldstein, 1984, p. 12).

In all the case study schemes, testing and marking are conducted by the candidate's own teacher, subject to specified conditions. In GOALS, staff were confident that results are independent of the particular teacher, and that other schools would mark in the same way. There is no moderation system for levels 1–3, but the reading and listening comprehension tests are composed of objective (multiple-choice) items, and in oral tests where marking is on a 3-point scale, detailed criteria are specified.

Harrison (1982) points out that 'examiner judgment is a perennial problem in all task-oriented tests unless the marking is done entirely objectively'. Clearly, marking in GOALS oral tests remains dependent on the experience, commitment, expertise and training of the teacher, but inter-marker reliability is assisted by scheme documents such as that quoted above. In KMP, where the tests are all written, marking schemes are provided which minimize the need for teacher judgment. In the SSC practical tests, some items require judgment in marking, but again detailed instructions are provided. There was no evidence in any of the case-study schools that marking is seen as a significant source of unreliability. Since the teachers are familiar with their pupils' work, it may be that this mediates their judgments during the tests in some instances, but it is not clear whether that would enhance or detract from reliability.

As Nuttall and Goldstein (1984) suggest, variation in test conditions may be a more salient source of unreliability. Such variations may arise from several factors which were identified during the case studies.

(1) Whether the test is concentrated in one session or held over several.

(2) The physical conditions of the test (for example whether the classroom is silent or noisy; whether the atmosphere is formal or informal).

(3) The degree of permissible assistance to the pupil during the test (for example encouragement during oral tests; information given by the teacher during practical tests; availability of workcards during KMP tests).

(4) Opportunities for pupils to cheat.

(5) Opportunities for pupils to re-take parts of the test after failure.

All these factors apply to one or more of the case study schemes, their relative importance varying according to the scheme. GOALS provides very detailed instructions for teachers on test administration, including notes on permissible assistance. SSC notes for teachers cover the setting-up of test stations, but as the case studies show there is considerable flexibility for schools to administer the tests as they wish. For example, there are no rules covering repetition of individual stations. Cheating appears to be a problem in KMP, and perhaps in SSC, but not in GOALS; where it does occur, test reliability is destroyed. The effects of the other four factors are less clear, but it may be supposed that they all affect test results to some extent. It seems desirable from the point of view of perceived fairness that schemes should define conditions for test administration which cover these factors.

However it could also be argued that greater specification of the conditions for test administration, although it might enhance reliability, would restrict the freedom of teachers to operate a scheme in the way they feel to be most suitable for the particular conditions in individual participating schools. One point that could be made is that if fairness is the reason for emphasis on test reliability, then other considerations should also be taken into account, for example available resources, the extent to which pupils are given specific test preparation, and the extent to which they are ready for tests (both cognitively and attitudinally). Secondly, the importance of reliability is dependent on the use to be made of test results. This point is made by Nuttall and Goldstein (1984), and also by Mortimore (1983) referring specifically to graded tests.

> If their principal use is formative — that is as a means of providing regular feedback on progress and diagnostic help to teachers — then questions of comparability and reliability, although important, may not be so critical. If, however, the main use is summative — providing a definitive statement of pupils' skills and attainment — then, in order for employers to give currency to the results, the reliability, validity and comparability issues cannot be avoided (Mortimore, 1983, p. 6).

Attitudes towards these technical issues may depend on whether graded tests are seen as high-quality teacher-made tests for internal assessment purposes or as an alternative to external examinations. In the former case there is perhaps little point in strictly controlling test conditions for reasons of reliability if this is at the expense of other objectives, for example pupil motivation, or the integration of curriculum and assessment. Many of those involved with graded-test schemes are far more concerned with the effects of the tests on classroom practice than they are with technical aspects of the tests, and may prefer to deal with any consequences of unreliability rather than to tackle its sources. Nevertheless it does seem necessary for public confidence in the schemes that the tests are seen to be fair, and in two of the case-study schemes (KMP and SSC) there is a case for reconsideration of the conditions of test administration with a view to possible further standardization.

It may be argued that reliability becomes more important if assessment is terminal than if the pupil is continuing to higher levels of the scheme. In the case of GOALS and KMP, those levels which are linked to public examinations become subject to the moderation procedures of the examination boards, which are designed to eliminate sources of unreliability, although public examinations are themselves not fully reliable (see, for example, Murphy, 1982). Mortimore (1983) expresses the view that 'To switch from an unreliable examination system to an unreliable graded test system, even if this could be justified on educational grounds, would be unfortunate' (p. 5). However, it seems unreasonable to expect a graded-test system, regarded as an alternative to external examinations, to be *more* reliable than the latter. There would then be a danger of reversion to the assessment only of those objectives for which we have managed to produce reliable tests. There may be reliability and moderation problems in the assessment of complex oral or practical tasks, but it has been suggested here that these problems need not be paramount.

A further reason for this is that the opportunity for parts of graded tests to be re-taken after failure (if it is in fact available to pupils) suggests that low reliability may not matter in the sense that one type of decision error (false failure) may be easily and rapidly corrected.* Graded test certificates do not attempt to assess the process of acquiring skills, only whether the skills have been acquired. Therefore the time taken to reach the mastery level is irrelevant, and the same certificate is awarded to a pupil who has passed at the first attempt or after several. In practice two or three attempts at the most are made, for logistic and motivational reasons as well as at least partial application of the principle of readiness in that pupils receive relevant instruction for the first attempt and remedial assistance for subsequent attempts.† It would be interesting to investigate whether there are differences between pupils who succeed at the first attempt and those who only succeed after initial failure, in attitude and motivation, in their ability to recall the mastered knowledge or repeat the mastered skills, or in predictive success at higher levels.

In this section it has been suggested that reliability of graded tests may be conceptualized in terms of fairness, and that marking is a lesser potential source of unreliability than variation in the conditions of test administration. Measures to standardize the latter may increase reliability, but may also have undesirable side effects in view of the nature and objectives of graded-test schemes.

Comparability

There has been no attempt to achieve, or claim, comparability between the various levels of graded test schemes in different subjects. Indeed Orr and Nuttall (1983) argue that 'the move towards criteria-referencing ... once and for all destroys the notion of subject comparability' (p. 23). Apart from the impossibility of making comparisons in criterion-referenced terms, schemes may be designed for different target groups, making norm-referenced comparisons equally impossible. In the case study schemes, level 1 is aimed at 11–12-year-old beginners in the case of GOALS, low-attaining 14–16-year-olds in the case of the science certificate, and upper primary pupils who have been studying mathematics for several years in the case of KMP. In theory, graded test schemes are age-independent, but in practice syllabuses and tests are written with particular groups in mind. There is no

---

*False success may be detected through inability to cope with material at the next level. However this only applies if pupils do continue with the scheme.

†Subsequent attempts are made at the *same* tests. Familiarity with the test items might make them easier, but would not necessarily do so.

consistency in the total number of levels in schemes in different subject areas, and this again makes clear that no comparability is intended. However, there might be a potential danger if several schemes were to be introduced into the same school that the use of the term 'level' could suggest comparability where none existed, to parents and others.

A second comparability issue is that of comparability over time. In the case-study schemes there have been few changes at a given level from year to year. Syllabus objectives, test items and pass criteria have tended to remain unaltered, although this may be due to a desire on the part of working parties of teachers to devote limited time and resources to developing further levels rather than any conscious wish to avoid problems of comparability over time. In SSC, some level 1 items have been replaced for the second year of operation of the scheme, but with no change of objectives or mastery levels. In GOALS, the recent revision of levels 1 and 2 (unchanged for six years) has been designed to meet certain criticisms, for example, of the complexity of oral testing. For many of the functions of all three case-study schemes (for example, curriculum reform, diagnosis, motivation) there appears to be no particular reason why 'standards' (however these are defined) need be held constant relative to each level. Indeed in some circumstances (for example, a high failure rate) it might be desirable for adjustments to be made. However, comparability over time might be thought to become more important if certificate descriptions are to be used for purposes of qualification or selection, or if graded-test levels are equated with public examination grades.

Further light may be cast on this argument by consideration of a third comparability issue, that of comparability between different graded-test schemes in the same subject area. The case studies do not provide direct evidence in the form of an example, but nevertheless suggest certain salient points. There is firstly the question of what it is that is being compared. Schemes may differ in target group, in the number and spacing of levels, in syllabus objectives, in the nature of the tests (for example a GOML scheme may or may not include a writing test), in their pass criteria (for example whether a single mastery level is defined, or whether there are hurdles or compensation) and in their success rates. It might not be easy to compare schemes with major differences in one or more of these attributes. It may be noted that even in the well-trodden paths of public examinations, comparability is not without its problems (Nuttall, 1979; Goldstein, 1982). 'The user should be aware of the vagueness of the concept of comparability, and the inevitable imprecision in our attempts to achieve it' (Nuttall, 1979, p. 17). Nuttall also argues that 'there is no way of investigating or attempting to achieve comparability other than relying on trained, but fallible human judgment'. But it would presumably be possible to set up a comparability study for graded-test schemes, perhaps a cross-moderation exercise as described by Johnson and Cohen (1983).

However, such a study would probably be beyond the resources of local groups, even if they felt it to be desirable. In any case, they might regard it as a diversion of effort from more useful activities, or resist any attempt to impose uniformity, even in the number of levels, on the grounds that graded tests should be appropriate for local conditions and follow, rather than lead, classroom practice. Nuttall and Goldstein (1984) state that 'The more standardization that is imposed on the quest for reliability and comparability, the greater the threat to the key features of graded tests' (p. 13).

As with the well-rehearsed case of public examinations, arguments for allowing variety in curricula are likely to clash with arguments for greater comparability of standards. It is difficult to see what action would or could be taken if a procedure were devised for determining comparability and significant differences between schemes were found, although the exercise might encourage groups to adopt features of other schemes if they were recognized to be superior to their own. Graded test schemes developed under the aegis of local authorities are not at present subject to any form of centralized control except in so far as they choose to become associated with the national examination system. With their emphasis on success for the great majority of pupils, schemes are not competitive and are therefore not concerned with the selection function, although certificate descriptions may be seen in terms of a qualification function.

It could be that to press for comparability would be to misunderstand the nature of graded tests by overemphasizing their possible application to selection. The reason for aiming at comparability between levels of different schemes would be to clarify the meaning of graded test results for selection purposes, and thereby change the present bias towards formative assessment functions (as demonstrated by the case study schemes). Nevertheless, interviewed teachers and pupils *were* concerned with both qualification and selection, and required national certification to be available. They saw GCE and CSE (and in future, GCSE) as the means of providing these functions, and this is the reason why both GOALS and KMP at higher levels were linked to public examinations. If graded tests were eventually to replace GCSE, the possibility of locally defined earlier levels and nationally defined later levels might have to be considered. At present it appears that comparability between different graded test schemes in the same subject area can safely be ignored except in the context of GCSE. It seems that we only need to compare schemes in order to compare individuals for selection purposes,*

---

*Although monitoring standards for accountability purposes might provide a further reason.

and to put this in further perspective, Nuttall (1979), in the context of public examinations, commented that 'For an individual candidate, lack of comparability pales into insignificance besides the inevitable inconsistency of the assessment process' (Nuttall, 1979, p. 17).

Chapter 7

The Relationship of Graded Tests to Other Assessment Initiatives in Britain

Multiple Solutions to the Same Problem?

The movement towards developing graded-test and graded-assessment schemes during the past fifteen or so years, has undoubtedly been motivated to a great extent by a growing dissatisfaction with traditional approaches to educational assessment and examining, and in some cases with the teaching methods that have been reinforced and perpetuated by such approaches. The curriculum area where there has been the greatest level of activity has been in modern languages, and many of the advocates of graded tests in this area have been quite open in terms of their opposition to traditional modern-language public examinations being at the heart of their concern to develop an alternative approach. Criticisms of public examinations from this quarter have generally mentioned some if not all of the following five points:

1. Examination syllabuses have been based on language structure (i.e. grammar) rather than on the use of language to communicate, and therefore have been inappropriate for most pupils.

2. Traditional examinations have had too long a time-span (up to five years) before any results have been achieved. Shorter-term objectives would, it is claimed, lead to a higher degree of motivation.

3. The use of norms to determine grade boundaries in public examinations has led to a sense of failure on the part of most candidates.

4. Public examination results have not reported clearly exactly what candidates can do.

5. Examinations have been designed only for the top 60 per cent of the ability range, and there has been no provision for the rest.

There is clearly quite a bit of overlap between this set of criticisms of public examinations and the list that we have developed, of qualities that are being looked for in new assessment initiatives, and which we presented in Chapter 1 (p. 11). In subsequent chapters we have attempted, through an examination of the case-study data, to explore the extent to which graded-test schemes that we selected to study have revealed evidence of measuring up to the demands of our list of qualities. This would require such schemes not only to provide an escape from the problems associated with public examinations but also genuinely enhance the attainment of curriculum aims. It should also turn educational assessment into a more harmonious and positive experience for both pupils and teachers. In many respects we feel that the data do provide sufficient support for such an analysis for the wider implications of the application of graded-test principles to be taken very seriously indeed. Of course there have been many problems as well as successes and our position is not one whereby we wish to unreservedly recommend the graded-test road as the one for everyone in education to go down! As with all educational developments there is a place for critical scrutiny. There are many aspects of a substantial move towards graded testing that would need further research and debate before it would be appropriate to implement such an approach. There are, however, clearly possibilities for considering this approach across the curriculum, perhaps as an alternative to GCSE or the system of national testing that may in the next few years be introduced along with a National Curriculum.

One thing that does appear to be certain is that there is a general wish to improve the quality of educational assessment in British secondary schools both in terms of the appropriateness of the assessments themselves, the meaningfulness of the results arising from them, and the impact that they have on teaching and the whole school curriculum. A central part of all of this has been an attempt to move more towards criterion-referenced assessment. This has involved assessors being more explicit about what skills and content areas are being assessed in any particular assessment as well as providing the users of the assessment results with more information about what they can understand successful candidates to have achieved in relation to what has been assessed. Many of the assessment initiatives have run into difficulty as they have moved in this direction, which is so attractive in theory but which tends to throw up fairly intractable problems in practice (Murphy, 1986). Much valuable experience in this area has been gained within the graded test and assessment movement, and even if such developments are to be eclipsed by their even more recent rivals, it is vitally important that the lessons that have been learned are taken account of by those who seek to take further the move towards more constructive and meaningful systems of pupil assessment.

At this stage in the discussion we will now turn to look specifically at developments within the new GCSE examination, the Records of Achievement Initiative, and the assessment scheme that has been proposed to accompany the new National Curriculum.

Graded Tests and the GCSE Examination

Given that the development of graded tests has been motivated to some considerable extent by a dissatisfaction with the former CSE and GCE O-level examinations, a key issue in relation to GCSE is the extent to which it has overcome some of the criticisms listed near the beginning of this chapter. Elsewhere we have argued (Murphy and Pennycuick, 1986; Murphy 1986 and 1988a) that, despite some of the rhetoric that has suggested otherwise, the GCSE has retained many of the undesirable features of the former examinations which it has replaced. Nevertheless it is also true that in some subject areas, modern languages being perhaps the best example, there is plenty of evidence to suggest that graded test developments have had a substantial influence on the construction of GCSE syllabuses and schemes of assessment. This in turn has led some GOML schemes to abandon their former practice of seeking Mode 3 status for their higher levels, within the new GCSE system, and merely enter their pupils for the Mode 1 GCSE assessments at that particular stage of their course.

Despite the evidence just referred to there are still plenty of voices of dissatisfaction being raised in relation to the nature of GCSE as the major secondary school assessment procedure, and some of these (for example, Warnock, 1985) are calling for a much wider development of graded tests in place of GCSE examinations.

However Page (1983) recognized that 'such satisfactorily radical solutions are unfortunately unlikely to be realised in the near future', and the decision to introduce GCSE in a climate of scepticism and widespread doubt confirms this view. In any case it could be argued that graded tests are not at present available in many subjects, and that where they are available they are often not sufficiently well established to command public confidence as a means of national certification. But it remains a long-term policy option to replace GCSE by a system of graded assessment.

A second possibility is for graded tests to be developed independently of public examinations, and to coexist with them. This is the situation in business studies, in physical education (where examinations are rare), and in music. It is also possible to include graded-test schemes as part of the assessment requirements for public examinations, particularly where the graded test becomes the practical or oral component. Nuttall (1984) refers to such a linkage model as *exempting* or *embedded*. Under such a system, graded assess-ments 'would give you exemption from part of the public examination or might be even more explicitly embedded within it' (Nuttall, 1984, p. 7). An example of embedding is given by the Kent Mathematics Project, where performance on KMP tests led to coursework grades for a Mode 3 CSE and a Mode 2 O-level examination.

A way for graded tests and public examinations to coexist without formal links (although syllabus compatibility may be necessary) is for the former to be aimed at lower age groups, or at the lower end of the ability range, or both. Thus a GOML scheme might be designed to be followed by pupils in the first three years of secondary school, and provide terminal certification for some pupils at the end of the third year, while other pupils go on to take public examinations. For some subjects, the option of dropp-ing the subject at age 14 is not available; the schemes for 'graduated' tests in mathematics arising from the proposals in the Cockcroft Report, and also the School Science Certificate scheme, have low-attaining 4th- and 5th-year pupils as their main target group. An issue for such schemes is that of status; they may suffer by being perceived as 'an option for the less able, those deemed incapable of being entered for the "real" examinations' (Harding, Page and Rowell, 1980, p. 88).

Nevertheless, for the bottom 40 per cent of the ability range, graded tests may provide the only possibility of certification of their achievements other than at purely school level. Certainly one policy option is for 'the top 60 per cent of 16-year-olds (whatever that means) to be entered for GCSE and 'the bottom 40 per cent' to take graded tests. However this possibility does not overcome the five criticisms of examinations listed above, and is unlikely to be acceptable to those whose main interest is in producing curricula which are more appropriate for less academic pupils.

In many cases pupils are unlikely to opt for graded tests at age 16 unless the resulting certificates carry status equivalent to public examinations. 'Teachers see it as their responsibility to pupils and parents to ensure that pupils' achievement is properly certificated and they are therefore unwilling to put the pupils' chances at risk' (Harrison, 1982, p. 46).

Further evidence for forging a link between graded assessment and 16+ certification is given by Newbould and Massey (1984). In a survey con-ducted for the Midland Examining Group project on the Assessment of Graded Objectives, they found that the overwhelming majority of those interviewed thought that graded assessments should be for all pupils within the secondary age range, and should provide a route to 16+ certification. 'Interviewees were often enthusiastic about the possibility of providing 16+ certification through a graded assessment system' (Newbould and Massey, 1984, p. 7). From the perspective of the GOML movement, Page (1983) recognizes that it is unrealistic to suppose that such a link can be avoided. 'From the beginning it was envisaged that a series of tests of graded objectives would eventually have to interlock in some way with the national examinations' (Page, 1983, p. 301).

One way in which this could be achieved is Nuttall's exempting or embedded model mentioned above. This suggests a strategy which may be worth further consideration by graded assessment schemes; some pupils could work on the syllabuses both for the scheme and the national examination simultaneously, while other pupils' work would be restricted to the graded assessments. The status of the latter, whilst not equal to that of the national examination, would be enhanced by being made a hurdle for that examination. An advantage of this strategy would be that graded assessment schemes could retain a considerable measure of independence, and therefore be able to adhere to principles based on the criticisms of traditional examinations stated at the beginning of this section.

The alternative linkage model given by Nuttall (1984) is a direct equivalence, single or multiple, between graded assessment levels and public examination grades. In the case of GCSE, he points out that 'the price for links will be that graded assessments will have to meet the national criteria' (Nuttall, 1984, p. 9).

The pressures of the former 16+ examination system and the need for graded tests to lead to some form of national certification have led many GOML schemes to negotiate with examination boards in order to establish higher graded-test levels as Mode 3 CSE or GCE examinations (see Harding, Page and Rowell, 1980). This requires compromise on principles of mastery and readiness, but enables the schemes to avoid restricting themselves to low-achieving pupils, or to younger age groups. For some of the graded assessment schemes currently under development, identification with examination grades is to be carried further. 'Some schemes state their intention to equate seven levels of test with the seven grades proposed for the reformed GCSE or "merged 16-plus", the two sets of grades matching each other one-to-one' (Pearce, 1983, p. 465). An example of such a scheme is GAIM, where GCSE is one of the factors taken into account to determine the total number of levels in the scheme (GAIM, 1985). Problems which arise with these direct equivalence models of linkage will be discussed in the next section.

It is clear that the relationship of graded assessment to public examinations is an important issue, which may modify the impact of these schemes on classroom learning; it is unrealistic to suppose that graded assessments at their present stage of development could on their own replace public examinations for 16-year-olds. Whether or not such a change comes about in the longer term will remain to be seen, and will depend partly on the extent to which the examination boards can respond to the alternative assessment philosophies being espoused by the supporters of the graded assessment movement, and by those involved in parallel developments such as profiles and records of achievement.

Identification of Graded Assessment Levels with Public Examination Grades

> It is of course true that there is a fundamental incompatibility between the national examinations, which are largely norm referenced and aim at dividing candidates into a rank order which enables a grade of pass to be awarded, and the graded objective tests which are intended to be criterion referenced. The fact that so many schemes have somehow managed to reconcile the two, shows how we can resolve contradictions in order to get something done. It is to be hoped this pragmatism has not cost too much in the way of distortion of the nature of graded objectives tests (Page, 1983, p. 302).

Incompatibility is hardly surprising, given that opposition to public examinations is a major reason for establishing graded-test schemes. However the norm-referenced/criterion-referenced distinction is a muddy one, both in the context of graded assessment (as we have seen earlier), and in the context of national examinations, which Christie and Forrest (1981) label as 'limen-referenced'. Nor is the question of discrimination between candidates clear, since some graded-test schemes provide more than one grade of success at a given level; the ABRSM exams offer three (pass, merit, distinction). This could be an example of the pragmatism referred to by Page, or indicate that the setting of a *single* cutting score on each test is not fundamental to graded test philosophy. We shall return to this point later. In the meantime, it seems that Page's incompatibility may be reduced to two elements, that national examinations have *too many* cutting scores, and that these cutting scores are determined *after the event* (at awarding meetings) whereas graded-test cutting scores are fixed beforehand.

Let us consider the five criticisms of examinations listed on p. 149 and see to what extent they could be overcome in the case of a GOML scheme (such as GOALS) which established level 4 as a Mode 3 CSE and level 5 as a Mode 3 O-level. The first criticism (inappropriate syllabuses) is resolved without difficulty, the only constraints on the graded-test scheme being the needs to present its syllabus and scheme of assessment in a form acceptable to the examination board, and to conform to established Mode 3 procedures. This may become more complicated with the introduction of GCSE because of the added need to satisfy the national criteria in modern languages, but the presence of supporters of graded objectives on the appropriate committees has influenced the style and content of these criteria, which are consistent with a communicative approach to language teaching.

The second criticism of public examinations (too long a time span) is easily met. Graded test schemes are largely free to specify levels which optimize the time span between tests, so that they occur sufficiently frequently to ensure continued motivation, while not too frequently to permit over-emphasis on testing. It is necessary to take account of the fact that different pupils will have different rates of progress, and it is likely that there will be smaller gaps, in terms of content and skills to be mastered, between lower levels than between higher levels of graded test schemes.

The third criticism (sense of failure) is less clear. In theory there is no pass/fail concept in GCSE, but in practice many who do not obtain Grades A, B or C may see themselves as failures, and be regarded in that light by employers and other users of this information. It is possible that Mode 3 examinations which are based on graded test schemes may produce a greater than usual proportion of candidates obtaining high grades, as a result of the operation of the principle of readiness, which may perhaps be used to justify skewed results to the examination boards. Of course the principle of readiness cannot be *strictly* adhered to, since public examinations are only available once, or at most twice, each year, but this seems to be of minor significance. Another factor which may be able to encourage a sense of success among candidates for these Mode 3 examinations is the opportunity to include test items with relatively high facility indices, although this is restricted by the requirement to produce a full range of grades. One possibility is for graded-test schemes to negotiate restricted-grade Mode 3 examinations, which might seem less inconsistent with the notion of a single level, although these might be unacceptable through status considerations. In any case the traditional awarding procedures of the public examinations appear to inhibit the emphasis on success aimed at by graded test schemes.

The fourth criticism is that public examination results do not clearly report what candidates can do. The reasons why it would be difficult for them to do so are discussed by Orr and Nuttall (1983) and again are related to existing grade awarding procedures. One problem is the practice of mark aggregation before grades are awarded, which enables candidates to compensate for poor marks in one part of an examination by doing well elsewhere. Another problem is the method of arriving at grade boundaries which 'relies on both norm-based and criteria-based considerations' (Orr and Nuttall, 1983, p. 13).

The desire for clear reporting is one reason why graded-test schemes often avoid any possible results other than 'pass' and 'fail'. The certificates issued to those who pass are frequently designed to include a list of the specific skills tested, and some indication of the standard required for a pass. Where several domains are tested, it may be preferable to insist that candidates reach a satisfactory standard in each, rather than merely requiring a specified aggregate score. If graded-test levels are identified with Mode 3 examinations, it would seem unlikely that the aim of clear reporting can be achieved unless the nettle of aggregation is firmly grasped, with hurdles on each part of the examination being separately specified for each grade. It would be much easier to avoid aggregation of marks in the case of a pass/fail test, where there is only one borderline to determine, than in a multi-grade examination.

Finally the fifth criticism (choice between GCSE and nothing) will be met to a large extent by graded test schemes which establish Mode 3 examinations. All pupils can participate in such schemes, up to whatever level they reach.

It is clear that major difficulties in identifying higher levels of GOML schemes with Mode 3 GCSE examinations are the wide range of grades available in the latter, and the methods by which the grade boundaries are determined. Nevertheless such identification has enabled some progress in overcoming the criticisms of public examinations which we have been considering. However it is worth bearing in mind Harrison's (1982) warning that 'there is a danger that using the graded test axe to chop down the public examination tree may risk blunting its cutting edge' (p. 48).

The edge could be blunted if too many compromises have to be made in order to conform to the examination system. But changes are currently taking place to both the axe and the tree. The concept of graded tests is broadening to that of graded assessment, and there is now a new species (or is it merely a hybrid?) of examination tree in the form of GCSE. It is probably too much to hope that in future the graded assessment movement might be regarded more as an organism in a symbiotic relationship with the tree, each conceding ground to the other for their mutual benefit.

A key issue is that of the pass/fail concept of graded assessment versus the range of grades in GCSE. One obvious way to reconcile the two is to identify graded assessment levels with individual grades, and this possible strategy of a one-to-one relationship in the context of GCSE will now be considered.

For GCSE before the introduction of grade criteria, all that is required to implement the strategy is for the concept of 'differentiation' to be carried to its logical conclusion by providing separate assessment for each grade. If this were to be done, GCSE would effectively *become* a graded assessment scheme, but there are several points to be considered. Firstly, level-progression in graded assessment usually implies extending the syllabus for each higher level; there are perhaps too many GCSE levels for this always to be feasible. Secondly there may be logistic difficulties in organizing separate assessments for every level. Thirdly, 'Graded objective levels represent different levels of achievement at *different stages* during the learner's course, whereas GCSE grades describe different levels of attainment at a *particular stage*, generally at 16+' (WJEC, 1985, p. 4).

This may require levels for GCSE and for graded assessment to be defined in different ways. Tuffnell (1985) points out that 'the domains appropriate to an "age-linked" examination (such as GCSE will essentially be) may well not be identical to those that the progression inherent within graded assessments might require' (p. 4). More generally, Nuttall (1984) asks 'Do we lose what is important within graded assessments if we have to meet the national criteria?' (p. 9).

The introduction of grade criteria will impose still more conditions, but could create an alternative to one-to-one or one-to-many relationships between graded assessment levels and GCSE grades. Draft grade criteria in several subjects are expressed in terms of a number of 'levels' (often four) in each domain, with final grades arrived at by a point-scoring system and aggregation, with some minimal hurdles (SEC, 1985 b). It may prove relatively straightforward to identify these levels with graded assessment levels, producing a 'many-to-many' relationship. However, since the future of grade criteria is uncertain (Murphy, 1986), we will not speculate further on their possible relationship to graded assessment, but leave this to future evaluation research. One question for such evaluation will be the extent to which the five criticisms of examinations stated at the beginning of this chapter are countered by whatever relationship emerges. In particular, clear reporting of GCSE results would appear to require the separate reporting (in some form of profile) of pupil performance on each domain, and this has been pointed out in the reports of the Grade Criteria Working Parties (SEC, 1985 b).

Graded Tests and Records of Achievement

At the time of writing this chapter the DES funded 'records of achievement' initiative has reached a critical stage and during 1988 it is expected that policy statements will be issued by the DES indicating the future direction for the national implementation of records of achievement involving all schools by 1990. The ESG funded pilot schemes, along with parallel initiatives in other LEAs around the country, have produced a wealth of experience of different approaches to pupil profiling, personal recording by pupils, and in some cases graded tests have been included as part of the battery of information that is used in putting together the overall record of achievement. The whole initiative has uncovered enormous divisions in terms of differing perceptions of profiling. In some cases there has been a complete change in teacher–pupil relationships as compared with other cases where profiling has been perceived as a minor modification in the production of school reports and references. It is only possible to speculate about what the DES policy statement will make of such diverse developments and experiences. The direction indicated by the National Curriculum assessment proposals, which we will be looking at briefly in the next sections may indicate that the more criterion-referenced style of record, which attempts to relate the achievement of individual children to prespecified curriculum goals, may be more likely to find favour than those at the pupil personal record of experience end of the spectrum. If this turns out to be the case then the chances of graded tests and related curriculum-goal oriented schemes of assessment playing a part in providing basic information for records of achievement is likely to be enhanced.

At this stage we will leave aside any further speculation about the future development of records of achievement as a national policy and reflect on the relationship between graded test and profiling experiences so far.

It is possible to regard profiling as the process of collection of assessment evidence and records of achievement as the presentation of that evidence in summative documents issued to pupils; here the word 'profile' will be used to refer to both. As with graded tests, the development of profiles in schools has often stemmed from dissatisfaction with the traditional external examination system (Garforth, 1984). Nuttall and Goldstein (1984) argue that

> The graded test movement shares many of the aims of the profiling movement, for example, a desire to ensure that education and assessment are seen as positive rather than negative experiences for all students, and a determination to put the curriculum first (Nuttall and Goldstein, 1984, p. 10).

Other common features include the use of a variety of assessment styles in order to allow a wider range of achievements to be assessed, and emphasis on the formative as well as the summative functions of assessment.

However it would be possible to carry the parallel between graded tests and profiles too far, and thus obscure the differences between them. Whereas graded tests may be regarded as assessment instruments, profiles are not the instruments themselves, but the provision of evidence from assessments (which may include graded assessments). In profiles, this evidence is broader, and typically presented in a more disaggregated form, than is the case with graded test results. It may extend to the assessment of attitudes, or to the collection and presentation of evidence relating to personal and social qualities. Unlike graded tests, profiles may emphasize the involvement of pupils in their own assessment by including provision for negotiated assessments and self-assessments. Indeed some proponents of profiles might argue that graded tests (and, more generally, graded assessments) do not go far enough in terms of radical assessment reform.

An issue common to the two movements has been whether they should be designed for the full ability range, or restricted to low-achieving pupils. While this is still an issue for graded assessment, in the case of profiles it appears to be generally accepted now that they should be for *all* pupils, and this is in fact government policy (DES, 1984).

A further issue is the assessment of cross-curricular skills. While profiling schemes do include subject assessments, many are also concerned with an attempt to identify skills which transcend existing subject boundaries. Graded tests are subject-based, and therefore help to maintain these boundaries. Although some tested skills (for example, measurement skills) may be cross-curricular in the sense that they occur in more than one subject area, nevertheless graded assessment is conducted within the context of the traditional subject curriculum. Graded tests do not (although perhaps they could) stress generalized skills such as the ability to follow a sequence of instructions, or to locate relevant information.

Doubts about the perceived inadequacies of graded assessment, as viewed from the perspective of the profiling movement, may be reinforced by other criticisms which have been referred to briefly in earlier sections. These are that graded assessment may be too rigid and stereotyped, with assessment dominating the curriculum even more than in traditional examinations.

> the worry of many is that graded tests will force assessment into the learning process . . . in a destructive way that will lead to an excess of testing and to a backwash effect throughout the secondary school or further education curriculum that will make the backwash effect of the much maligned systems of examination at 16+ look mild in comparison (Nuttall and Goldstein, 1984, p. 12).

Such undesirable backwash effects may include excessive 'teaching to the test', and learning restricted to the tested tasks, without generating the ability to undertake new tasks or encouraging exploration beyond the specified syllabus. Curricula may tend to become directed primarily towards skills or tasks which can be clearly specified, and away from areas (for example literature) where it may be less easy to define objectives. It should be noted that many of the graded assessment schemes under development are aware of these dangers, and plan to counteract them, for example by the inclusion of investigatory work in mathematics. Nevertheless it might be felt that profiling offers a degree of flexibility which is not possible in graded assessment. OCEA (see pp. 110–1) is an example of a profiling project which has moved away from graded assessment as such, and other developments (for example, the Dorset/SREB Assessment and Profiling Project) have no plans to include it.

However, an alternative response is to emphasize the positive features of graded assessment, to accept that it satisfies aims for subject-based assessment, and that it may be preferable to alternatives for that. This response would support the inclusion of graded assessment both in the formative profiling process and as a component of summative records of achievement. An example of a large-scale development following this approach is that in London (see pp. 108–10) where the graded assessments in the five selected subject areas are intended to contribute towards a 'London Record of Achievement' to be issued to school leavers in all ILEA schools, a proposal which is supported by the Hargreaves Report (ILEA, 1984).

Graded Tests and Modular and Unit Assessments

Another broad area of current interest, the concept of modular curricula (Warwick, 1987), linked with a unit credit system of assessment, is relatively new in secondary schools, although it is well established in further and higher education. Such a system is to be developed for ILEA schools as a result of proposals in the Hargreaves Report (ILEA, 1984), and another scheme under the aegis of the Northern Examining Association is also at the early stages of development (NEA, 1985). Along rather different lines is a system of modular assessment for the Somerset TVEI scheme (Adams and Wilmut, 1985). It is too early to predict the outcomes of these developments, but the question arises as to the extent to which unit credit schemes are compatible with graded assessment. In practice the question of compatibility is only significant in subject areas for which graded assessment schemes exist, and one advantage of unit credits is that they may be suitable for a much wider range of subjects, and indeed for a multi-disciplinary approach to curriculum design. (For a fuller discussion of this point, see Murphy and Torrance, 1988).

Both unit credits and graded assessment fall under the heading of 'staged assessment' (SEC, 1984), and aim to provide short-term goals for pupils, together with work at an appropriate level of difficulty. Both are subject to the constraints imposed by parameters of the school timetable, but ideally there would be flexibility for pupils to change from one subject to another after having reached a certain stage, or to repeat a level or a unit if they have failed to reach a satisfactory standard. The possibility of increasing such flexibility by vertical timetabling has been considered earlier.

In a recent conference paper (ULSEB, 1985c) it is stated that, in London, graded assessments and unit credits are not seen as incompatible and that graded assessment schemes will probably be flexible enough to be implemented in a unit credit organization.

> Nevertheless some tensions exist, arising mainly from the graded assessment focus on the developing repertoire of concepts and skills of individual students ('assessing when ready') in contrast to the unit credit requirements of standard teaching units with common objectives for a range of students. (ULSEB, 1985c, p. 2)

Units (or modules) are designed to occupy a given, fixed period of time (in the case of the Hargreaves Report recommendations, half a term). This is in contrast to the notion in graded assessment that pupils spend varying lengths of time on particular levels, according to their abilities and efforts, with no time limit. But, as we have seen, the principle of readiness is not always easy to apply, so that in practice it may be possible to resolve the apparent contradiction between graded assessment and unit credits, although it is difficult to see how this could be done in the case of a fully individualized graded test scheme such as the Kent Mathematics Project. Another consideration is that half a term is much shorter than the time spent by pupils in mastering each level of *any* graded test scheme, but it may be possible to subdivide graded test levels into convenient units, thereby overcoming the problem for modular curriculum design that different subjects have different numbers of levels occupying differing periods of pupil time. Existing work on graded assessment may be of assistance in quantifying the difficulty of units within a modular system, and thus helping to overcome the problem of what weights to attach to individual unit credits if some system of credit accumulation is envisaged.

However, although it may be possible to reconcile graded assessment with unit credits, a note of caution should perhaps be sounded. In the face of the present bewildering array of assessment initiatives and the resources, internal reorganization and in-service training needed to introduce them, it may be preferable for schools (or LEAs) to be selective, and restrict their involvement to manageable proportions. With so much development work going on there must also be a temptation for local policy-makers to adopt a 'wait-and-see' attitude.

Graded Tests and the Assessment of the National Curriculum

The recent proposals (DES, 1987) for a National Curriculum contain almost as much about the assessment arrangements that are to accompany it as they do about the content of the curriculum. Undoubtedly this reinforces the view of Hargreaves (1987) that assessment reform has been recognized by politicians as a very powerful vehicle for curriculum reform.

There has already been widespread criticism of the assessment proposals for testing all children in all areas of the National Curriculum at the ages of 7, 11, 14 and 16 (Murphy, 1987, 1988b), and we won't go over all of the aspects of that debate here. It is however instructive to consider the considerable extent to which, once again, another new assessment initiative has been proposed that seeks to achieve much that has already been achieved through graded tests, and yet pays little or no attention to the possibility of making use of existing graded-test schemes or even drawing on the experiences gained through them. It seems that again an attempt may be made to re-invent the wheel in this respect, and the description of the assessment programme, which is contained in the consultation document (DES, 1987) will be read with much ironical laughter by those who have sought to achieve some of the objectives of the proposed programme of assessments and have learnt through experience just how impossible it is to put such laudable ideals into practice.

Probably the greatest conflict between the graded test developments and the National Curriculum testing programme, which is being proposed, concerns the insistence on sticking to strict age-related targets of achievement in relation to the National Curriculum. It is apparently thought that this is important in terms of the accountability motives that appear to be driving these particular curriculum and assessment proposals. The idea of setting attainment targets for all 11 year olds in mathematics, say, which are realistic and which will stretch every child *and* which will lead to improved standards of achievement throughout the country sounds like recognizable political rhetoric and very poor educational theory and practice. Certainly the observation in the Cockcroft Report that the mathematical achievements of 11 year olds varied by a span of at least seven years is difficult to reconcile with the advice given by the Secretary of State to the Mathematics and Science National Curriculum Working Groups that 'So far as possible I want to avoid having different attainment targets for children of different levels of ability' (Kenneth Baker, Guidance for Curriculum Working Groups, 24 August 1987).

There are many aspects of the proposals that appear to make little sense in terms of it being possible to put them into practice as viable assessment procedures. As with GCSE (Murphy, 1988a) a lot of faith is being placed in the notion of 'differentiated assessment', whereby pupils whose achievement levels are very different are supposed to be able to demonstrate these levels within the same single system of assessment. Laudable as this idea may be, there is little evidence that anyone has actually come up with an assessment procedure which does any such thing. It really is inevitable that any known method of assessment that is applied to an entire cohort of children of a particular age will almost certainly be far too easy for some and far too difficult for others. Thus the idea that the proposed national testing programme will stretch every child towards realistic targets is just a more acceptable way of saying that targets will be set which some will be able to pass standing on their heads and others won't get within a million miles of achieving.

The graded test movement has been all about setting up attainment targets, as it happens, in quite a number of the key areas in the National Curriculum. The difference in the assessment philosophy however has been a recognition that pupils will reach a point when they are ready to attempt to demonstrate that they have reached these targets at different rates. Thus movement through the levels and entry for these tests has been on the basis of progress rather than age. This we would contend has been beneficial in preserving a positive attitude towards the tests as a means of demonstrating, more formally, attainments that are already thought to have been reached.

Our fear in relation to the national curriculum attainment targets is that they could become gargoyles decorating but quite irrelevant to a curriculum for which they are intended to be cornerstones. More worrying still is that to extend the analogy further, they may quickly become millstones around the necks of teachers and pupils, reinforcing a sense of failure and dragging them down in their own progress towards the achievements within the national curriculum framework of which they are more than capable.

Graded tests and assessments could play a key role in an alternative approach to assessing the national curriculum. However if that is to happen there will have to be a considerable revision of the guidelines that have already been put forward by the Secretary of State, in his letter (of 24 August 1987) to the Mathematics and Science National Curriculum Working Groups, from which we have already quoted.

Graded Tests and National Graded-Assessment Projects

As we pointed out in Chapter 1 this book has looked mainly at local graded-test schemes in action and has paid much less attention to the larger-scale graded-assessment schemes, many of which were at the time of the research, and still are, more at a stage of development than implementation. These projects are characterized by early involvement of institutions such as LEAs and examination boards in the development work, and by levels of funding which allow the appointment of a full time project team, often including seconded teachers. This may lead to an approach which is more 'professional' and theoretical than that of (say) a local GOML group, since a fuller justification of decisions and actions may be required, but there is a danger that these schemes may become too ambitious in scope and hence unrealistic in practice in schools. Several of these centralized schemes are designated as feasibility studies, perhaps in recognition of this danger. Established fully operational schemes have the justification that they 'work' in practice, and one measure of their success is their take-up rate in schools. Another potential danger of these centralized schemes is that they may be imposed upon school departments which are unsympathetic towards graded assessment or its associated curricular philosophy by authorities with a vested interest in promoting these developments. There is a need for evaluation studies of such centralized projects, but these will have to overcome the problem of identifying and isolating initial effects of individual schemes and will then have to face the question of what will be the impact of a possible proliferation of schemes.

There are many differences between a locally based graded-test scheme involving, say, twenty schools, most if not all represented on the working parties, and one of the national schemes currently under development. It follows that there is a limit to the degree to which ideas and methods can be transferred from one to the other. One factor is that subject departments decide to adopt, or not to adopt, local schemes; teachers may drop out of the working parties if they feel unsympathetic towards the developments taking place. With centralized schemes, even if departments are enthusiastic about the scheme, individual teachers cannot have the same opportunity to contribute to the development of syllabuses and assessment procedures, since this is done centrally. These schemes are likely to be developed by teams of professional curriculum developers and seconded teachers, who have a contractual commitment, whereas local schemes are developed by advisers and practising teachers, whose commitment is voluntary. Apart from motivational considerations, one possible effect is for centralized graded-assessment schemes to be more ambitious and complex than existing graded-test schemes. A higher quality may be attainable by centralized schemes, with their greater resources, but inevitably teachers will lose 'ownership' of the schemes, and what is proposed may create even more problems of implementation in the long term than do LEA-based graded test schemes. A further point is that centralized schemes have to satisfy far more groups of stake-holders; in addition to the participating schools there may be examination boards, a contributing university and several LEAs involved in the development work, as well as seconded teachers on the working parties.

The role of examination boards or examining groups in the development of graded assessment deserves consideration. Problems of such involvement include the following.

1. Traditional attitudes and practices. One wonders whether the boards are sufficiently flexible to adopt the philosophy of graded assessment, or whether they will regard it simply as a form of GCSE, to be handled as far as possible in the same way.

2. Their remoteness from schools. They are perceived by teachers as external agencies.

3. Their need to generate income, either by entry fees, or by direct funding from LEAs, or by royalties on published materials.

4. The importance to them of summative assessment functions, and hence of technical considerations such as those of moderation and/or accreditation for large-scale candidature.

Examining groups are likely to want early GCSE equivalence for the graded assessment schemes which they sponsor, and thus to favour a top-down approach, in contrast with the bottom-up development of existing graded test schemes, which have taken several years to build up to Mode 3 CSE and GCE examinations. The greater resources and expertise available to examining groups may enable progress to be more rapid, but this is cancelled, at least to some extent, by the greater complexity of their proposals, and in some cases by the desire to first establish new curriculum models.

Harrison (1982, p. 49) considers the possibility of a new role for the examination boards, and suggests that they could, if they wished, 'begin to act as a service to teachers involved in assessment'. He gives several possibilities for the forms this service might take, including

1. provision of programming facilities for local test statistics;

2. central storage of material in computer files;

3. printing of selected test materials on demand;

4. centralized amendment of materials in the light of experience and review.

If this sort of approach were to be adopted by the boards, it would be possible for graded-test schemes to remain on a local basis, and to retain a high degree of participation, while the boards contributed a great deal towards easing the administrative load and increasing the efficiency and quality of the schemes. The principal problem for the examination boards would appear to be in devising a form of certification based on student performance on locally based graded assessment schemes but acceptable in a national context.

Future Decision-Making about Assessment Strategies

Any discussion about education assessment has the potential to turn quickly into a discussion about curriculum aims and priorities. This in turn can move on to an even broader discussion about what education is for, and the constraints we might want to place on schooling, its organization and the way children are guided through it. This we regard as an entirely healthy debate, and one which should not be allowed to be suppressed by a much more narrowly defined discussion about whether one assessment approach is better than another based purely on the technical attributes of the two schemes.

We would argue that the graded-test movement has made a sizeable contribution to thinking about the organization and practice of educational assessment in secondary schools. Just how far the positive aspects of this experience can be harnessed to emerging thinking about curriculum aims and priorities remains to be seen. We also hold the view that searching questions should be asked about any new assessment initiative that could, if allowed to grow, dominate secondary education in the way that public examinations at 16+ have for so long.

We are by no means alone in thinking that these questions should include as a major focus enquiry into the broader effects of such an initiative. For example, Goldstein and Nuttall (1986) adopt a similar position. From a very different perspective, Hargreaves (1987) also looks at emerging assessment initiatives such as graded tests and attempts to discuss them in relation to their curricular and social implications. He raises a number of questions specifically about graded tests, which are predicated on a belief that current assessment initiatives are a favoured political route (of the present government) for invading the once 'secret garden' of the school curriculum. In summary, these questions are:

1. Will the reported increased pupil motivation drop off once the currency of graded-test certificates is discovered to be of low value? And will the

value of the currency drop even further if more and more parts of the curriculum start using it?

2. Could the perceived benefits of shortening the previously distant horizons of educational success lead pupils and teachers into a world where they also lose sight of the intrinsic purpose and validity of what is being taught and learned? Similarly could the chase after so many short-term goals and certificates become so confusing to pupils and parents that they are in danger of being sucked into an even more sinister system of selection, where pupils are channelled into curriculum routes leading to very limited educational and employment horizons without ever becoming aware of what is happening to them?

3. Is another dimension of curriculum control, inherent in graded test and assessment developments, to be perpetuated through a restriction of such developments within conventional high-status subject areas such as mathematics, science, modern languages and English? Will this further marginalize areas of study falling outside the main subject specializations, such as environmental education, world studies and political education?

4. Will the deception of pupils, who might unknowingly be led down a graded test dead-end street be further exacerbated if such tests are 'out-flanked' by GCSE, and thus become relegated as a low-status cooling-out route for the 'less able'?

These are all major questions which need to be considered by anyone concerned to build the graded-test experience, reported in this book, into a vehicle for improving the quality of schooling and in particular for introducing innovation into the curriculum as an attempt to increase pupil motivation and achievement. Some aspects of Hargreaves' questions have been considered in this book, but a full discussion would lead us into much wider arguments on issues to do with a sociological analysis of the curriculum than we can enter into here. The debate about where overall assessment policy should now go is one which we have attempted to inform, but are not going to attempt to end!

At the time of writing the position is in one sense very healthy as assessment initiatives are springing up rapidly and are attracting more and more attention. Unfortunately many of them appear to be destined to be short-lived as they are quickly outflanked by rival initiatives. This may be particularly disheartening for those hard-pressed teachers who in many cases have invested a lot of time and energy in their development. At present we have GCSE, records of achievement and profiles, CPVE and a range of other pre-vocational qualifications, graded tests and assessments, modular and unit credit systems, all competing for similar aspects of the assessment of secondary school pupils. Within months all of these developments are likely to be overshadowed, or perhaps in some cases re-styled, in terms of the national system of tests to which we have already referred.

The most satisfactory way, in our view, that such a confusing situation could be resolved would be for future thinking about assessment to be based much more closely on an agreed view of the school curriculum and what we want children to experience as they go through it. That would be no mean task as the current largely political invasion of the secret garden of the school curriculum has already turned into something more akin to a rampage in a set of public allotments, with individual groups attempting to operate their own cultivation methods, on their own plots, in the face of plans to plough the whole area up in order to plant a cash crop (TVEI?), preceded by occasional visits from low-flying aircraft releasing what could be fertilizers, pesticides or even more powerful inorganic interventions. Even if a certain variety in growing methods survives it now seems probable that national guidelines for assessment will be used as a means of controlling and monitoring productivity levels and crop yield.

As too many schemes compete with each other, few can really expect to survive in anything other than a marginal position. Apart from considering which is likely to come out on top in this battle for survival, a further dimension to the analysis of graded tests in relation to other assessment initiatives is the consideration of the common ground and experience that exists between these various alternatives. Already we have seen graded-test schemes having been given CSE and GCE O-level equivalent status and, in the case of modern languages, this has apparently led in turn to a very considerable influence on the development of GCSE syllabuses. Similarly graded test and assessment schemes have featured as a prominent part of some of the records of achievement pilot schemes, notably in OCEA, London and the 'Northern Partnership'. On top of all this it is surely inevitable that as the debate about assessing age-related attainment targets within the National Curriculum takes off, there will be further opportunities for considerable lessons to be learned from the now well-established experience of some graded-test schemes.

Will Graded Tests have an Impact in the Future?

The three LEA-based graded-test schemes that we have studied in this book, represent much of what has been good about locally organized curriculum and assessment initiatives. Each has been based on a good deal of school-focused activity with appropriate support from LEA advisory staff. The involvement of such individuals to promote and sustain the development has been critical and reinforces a view expressed by Stenhouse (1975) in terms of their role in school-based innovation: 'Local advisory staffs are probably critical for the improvement of schools . . . they are clearly key figures in innovation' (p. 187).

Whether such a model can be expected to continue into the future depends a great deal on the outcome of major proposals for reorganizing the education system, which are still being debated as this book goes to press. It is quite unclear what place there will be for school-based innovation within a national curriculum framework, and the role of LEAs and LEA advisers could quickly change with advisers taking on more of an inspectorial function in relation to policing the national curriculum. Similarly as we have discussed earlier in this chapter graded tests could play an extremely significant role as part of a revised assessment programme to accompany the national curriculum, but on the other hand they could be squeezed more or less completely out of existence by a system of age-related testing at 7, 11, 14 and 16.

Whatever happens in the future we now regard the graded-test movement as an extremely valuable educational development, which has done much to put into practice ideals of making pupil assessment a much more positive part of secondary-school education. If it only remains as part of the history of secondary schooling in Britain in the 1970s and 1980s, it will stand as a very good example of the harnessing together of curriculum aims and assessment methods to enhance the educational experience and achievements of large numbers of secondary-school pupils.

References

ADAMS, R.M. and WILMUT, J. (1985) 'The Somerset TVEI scheme: an approach to modular assessment', Paper presented at the BERA conference, Sheffield, September 1985.

Associated Board of the Royal Schools of Music (1983) *Summary of the 94th annual report of the Board for the year 1982*, London: ABRSM.

BAKER, Kenneth (1987) 'Guidance for Curriculum Working Groups', 24 August, 1987.

BANKS, B. (1985) 'Ed tech from programs to material-bank in the KMP', *Programmed Learning and Educational Technology* 22(1), pp. 57–62.

BARDELL, G., FEARNLEY, A. and FOWLES, D. (1984) *Joint Research into Criterion-Referencing of Grades at 16+: The Contribution of Graded Objective Schemes in Mathematics and French*, Joint Matriculation Board and Schools Council, Manchester.

BLACK, H.D. and DOCKRELL, W.B. (1980) *Diagnostic Assessment in Secondary Schools*, Edinburgh: Scottish Council for Research in Education.

BLOOM, B.S. (1976) *Human Characteristics and School Learning*, New York: McGraw-Hill.

BROADBENT, J. and MEHTA, M. (1985) 'Graded objectives for community languages?' *Education Journal*, January 1985, pp. 9–10.

BROADFOOT, P. (1979) *Assessment, Schools and Society*, London: Methuen.

—— (ed., 1984) *Selection, Certification and Control*. Lewes: Falmer Press.

BROWN, Margaret (1983) 'Graded tests in Mathematics: the implications of various models for the Mathematics curriculum', Paper presented at BERA conference, London, September 1983.

BROWN, Sally (1981) *What do they know? A Review of Criterion-Referenced Assessment*. Scottish Education Department. Edinburgh: HMSO.

BUCKBY, M. *et al.* (1981) *Graded Objectives and Tests for Modern Languages: an Evaluation*, London: Schools Council.

BURGESS, T. and ADAMS, E. (1980) *Outcomes of Education*, London: Macmillan.

CHRISTIE, T. and FORREST, G.M. (1981) *Defining Public Examination Standards*. Schools Council Research Studies, London: Macmillan Education.

COLE, I. (1984) 'An evaluation of the Kent Mathematics Project "L" materials', *Remedial Education* 19(1), pp. 34–6.

DES (1982) *Mathematics Counts*. Report of the Committee of Inquiry into the

Teaching of Mathematics in Schools (The Cockcroft Report), London: HMSO.

—— (1983) 'Records of Achievement for School Leavers', Draft Policy Statement, Department of Education and Science.

—— (1984) *Records of Achievement: A Statement of Policy*, Department of Education and Science/Welsh Office.

—— (1987) *The National Curriculum 5–16. A Consultation Document*, London: HMSO.

DUNNING, R. (ed., 1983) *French for Communication: The East Midlands Graded Assessment Feasibility Study*, University of Leicester School of Education.

FREEDMAN, E.S. (1982) *Evaluation of the East Midlands Graded Assessment Feasibility Study for the Year 1979–80*, University of Leicester School of Education.

—— (1983) 'Evaluation of the feasibility study', in R. Dunning (Ed.) *French for Communication: the East Midlands Graded Assessment Feasibility Study*, University of Leicester School of Education.

GAIM (1983) *Newsletter 1*, Graded Assessment in Mathematics Project, King's College, London.

—— (1985) *Newsletter 3*, Graded Assessment in Mathematics Project, King's College, London.

GAGNE, R.M. (1968) 'Learning hierarchies', *Educational Psychologist*, 6, pp. 1–9.

GARFORTH, D. (1984) 'Profiles: the state of play', in D. Garforth and H. Macintosh (eds) *Curriculum and Assessment*, Report of the first annual conference, Dorset/SREB Assessment and Profiling Project, July 1984.

GOLDSTEIN, H. (1982) 'Models for equating test scores and for studying the comparability of public examinations', *Educational Analysis* 4(3), pp. 107–18.

GOLDSTEIN, H. and NUTTALL, D.L. (1986) 'Can graded assessments, records of achievement and modular assessment co-exist with the GCSE?' in Gipps, C. (ed.) *The GCSE: An Uncommon Examination* Bedford Way Papers 29, University of London Institute of Education.

GRONLUND, N.E. (1973) *Preparing Criterion-Referenced Tests for Classroom Instruction*, New York: Macmillan.

HMI (1983) *Report by HM Inspectors on a Survey of the Use of Graded Tests of Defined Objectives and Their Effect on the Teaching and Learning of Modern Languages in the County of Oxfordshire*, Department of Education and Science.
(1985 a) *Report by HM Inspectors on Classroom Practice in Schools in NW England Preparing Pupils for Graded Tests of Defined Objectives in Modern Languages*, Department of Education and Science.

—— (1985 b) *Report by HM Inspectors on a Survey of Work in Modern Languages in 27 Schools in the Leeds Metropolitan District Taking Graded Tests of Defined Objectives in Modern Languages*, Department of Education and Science.

HARDING, A., PAGE, B. and ROWELL, S. (1980) *Graded Objectives in Modern Languages*, London: Centre for Information on Language Teaching and Research (CILT).

HARGREAVES, A. (1987) 'Educational Assessment — a test for socialism', Paper presented at a World Wildlife funded Conference on 'Ecology, Development and Education'.

HARGREAVES, D.H. (1982) *The Challenge for the Comprehensive School*. London: Routledge and Kegan Paul.

HARRISON, A. (1982) *Review of Graded Tests*, Schools Council Examinations

Bulletin 41, London: Methuen Educational.

—— (1985) 'Graded Assessment', in *E206 Block 4. Supplementary Reading*, Milton Keynes: Open University.

HORNE, S.E. (1983) 'Learning hierarchies: a critique', *Educational Psychology* 3(1), pp. 63–77.

HOUSTON, J.G. (1983) 'Norm and criterion referencing of performance levels in tests of educational attainment', Draft paper, Associated Examining Board, Aldershot.

ILEA (1984) *Improving Secondary Schools*, Report of the Committee on the Curriculum and Organization of Secondary Schools, chaired by Dr David H. Hargreaves, ILEA.

JOHNSON, S. and COHEN, L. (1983) *Investigating Grade Comparability Through Cross-moderation*, London: Schools Council.

JONES, J.E.M. (1984) The uses employers make of examination results and other tests for the selection of 16–19 year olds for employment, M.Phil. thesis, University of Reading.

Kent Mathematics Project (KMP) (1978) *KMP Teachers' Guide Levels 1–4*, London: Ward Lock Educational.

—— (1981) *Test Answer Books*, London: Ward Lock Educational.

KIMBERLEY, K. (1984) 'Broken English', *Times Educational Supplement*, 10 February 1984, p. 23.

London Regional Examining Board (1982) 'Graded tests', Discussion paper for extended meeting of Secretaries, London, November 1982.

MEG (undated) 'On the level', Project document, the Midland Examining Group Project on Assessment of Graded Objectives, Cambridge.

MORTIMORE, J. and MORTIMORE, P. (1984) *Secondary school examinations: 'the helpful servants, not the dominating master'* Bedford Way Papers 18, University of London Institute of Education.

MORTIMORE, P. (1983) 'Graded tests: a challenge or a problem?', Paper presented at BERA conference, London, September 1983.

MURPHY, R.J.L. (1982) 'A further report of investigations into the reliability of marking of GCE examinations', *British Journal of Educational Psychology* 52, pp. 58–63.

—— (1986) 'The emperor has no clothes: grade criteria and the GCSE' in Gipps, C. (ed.) *The GCSE: An Uncommon Exam*, Bedford Way Papers, University of London Institute of Education.

—— (1987) 'Assessing a national curriculum' in *Journal of Education Policy* 2(4), 317–23.

—— (1988a) 'The Birth of GCSE', in Hargreaves, A. and Reynolds, D. (eds) *Educational Policy Initiatives*, Lewes: Falmer Press.

—— (1988b) 'Great Education Reform Bill Proposals for Testing—a Critique' *Local Government Studies* (in press).

MURPHY, R.J.L. and PENNYCUICK, D.B. (1985) 'Evaluating current initiatives in educational assessment: Graded Assessments and GCSE', Paper presented to the Nuffield Assessment Seminar Group. London, 15 November 1985.

—— (1986) 'Graded assessment and the GCSE' in T. Horton (ed.) *GCSE: Examining the New System*, London: Harper Row.

MURPHY, R.J.L. and TORRANCE, H. (1988) *The Changing Face of Educational Assessment* Milton Keynes: Open University Press.

NEA (1985) Pre-conference paper from the NEA/LEA group for conference on Records of Achievement: Practical Issues, at Manchester University, January 1985, Northern Examining Association.

NFER (1985) *GT Newsletters Numbers Three and Four*, Graduated Tests in Mathematics Project, National Foundation for Educational Research, Slough.

NEWBOULD, C.A. and MASSEY, A.J. (1984) 'Initial survey of views on aspects of graded assessment', Report for the Project on the Assessment of Graded Objectives, Midland Examining Group.

NICHOLLS, J.G. (1984) 'Conceptions of ability and achievement motivation', in R. Ames and C. Ames (eds) *Research on Motivation in Education. Volume 1: Student Motivation*, Orlando, Florida: Academic Press.

NUTTALL, D.L. (1979) 'The myth of comparability' *Journal of the National Association of Inspectors and Educational Advisers* 11, pp. 16–18.

—— (1984) 'Alternative assessments: only connect . . .' in SEC *New Approaches to Assessment*, Seminar Report, 13 June 1984.

NUTTALL, D.L. and GOLDSTEIN, H. (1984) 'Profiles and graded tests: the technical issues', in *Profiles in Action*, London: FEU.

OCEA (1983) *Newsletters 1 and 2*, University of Oxford Delegacy of Local Examinations.

—— (1984) *Newsletter 4*, University of Oxford Delegacy of Local Examinations.

—— (1985) *Newsletter 5*, University of Oxford Delegacy of Local Examinations.

ORR, L. and NUTTALL, D.L. (1983) *Determining Standards in the Proposed Single System of Examining at 16+*. Comparability in Examinations Occasional Paper 2, Schools Council, London.

PAGE, B. (1983) 'Graded objectives in modern language learning', *Language Teaching* 16(4), pp. 292–308.

—— (1985) 'With a few good friends', *Times Educational Supplement*, 1 February 1985.

PARLETT, M. and HAMILTON, D. (1976) 'Evaluation as illumination', in D. Tawney (ed.) *Curriculum Evaluation Today: Trends and Implications*, Schools Council, London: Macmillan.

PEARCE, J. 'The future of graded tests', *Education*, 17 June 1983, pp. 465–6.

PENNYCUICK, D.B. (1983) 'What is a graded test?' Discussion paper, University of Southampton Department of Education.

—— (1984) 'The place of options in graded test schemes', Discussion paper, University of Southampton Department of Education.

—— (1985) 'What has Australia to offer the graded test movement?', *Westminster Studies in Education* 8, pp. 65–76.

—— (1986) The development, use and impact of graded tests, with particular reference to modern languages, mathematics and science. Unpublished PhD thesis, University of Southampton.

PENNYCUICK, D.B. and MURPHY, R.J.L. (1986 a) 'The impact of the graded test movement on classroom teaching and learning', *Studies in Educational Evaluation* 12(3), 275–279.

—— (1986 b) 'Mastery, validity and comparability issues in relation to graded assessment schemes', *Studies in Educational Evaluation* 12(3), 305–11.

PILLINER, A.E.G. (1979) 'Norm-referenced and criterion-referenced tests – an evaluation', in *Issues in Educational Assessment*, Scottish Education

Department, Edinburgh.

POPHAM, W.J. (1978) *Criterion-Referenced Measurement*, Eaglewood Cliffs, NJ: Prentice-Hall.

RUTHERFORD, W.L. (1979) 'Criterion-referenced programmes: the missing element', *Journal of Curriculum Studies* 11(1), pp. 47–52.

SEC (1984) *New Approaches to Assessment*, Seminar Report, 13 June 1984, Secondary Examinations Council.

—— (1985 a) *Differentiated Assessment in GCSE*, Working Paper 1, Secondary Examinations Council, London.

—— (1985 b) *Draft Grade Criteria*, Reports of the Working Parties, Secondary Examinations Council, September 1985.

SSCC (1984) *Information Sheet 3*, SMP – Suffolk – Chelsea – COSSEC: Graduated Assessment in Mathematics, A study commissioned by the Department of Education and Science.

Secondary Mathematics Individualized Learning Experiment (1980) *SMILE*, Introductory booklet issued by the SMILE Centre, Middle Row School, Kensal Road, London W10 5DB.

STENHOUSE, L. (1975) An Introduction to Curriculum Research and Development, London: Heinemann.

TATTERSALL, K. (1983) *Differentiated examinations: a strategy for assessment at 16+?*, Schools Council Examinations Bulletin 42, London: Methuen Educational.

TUFFNELL, R. (1985) 'Levels of attainment in graded assessment schemes and other new forms of assessment and links with GCSE', Paper presented at a conference on Records of Achievement: Practical Issues, at Manchester University, January 1985, on behalf of the Midland Examining Group.

ULSEB (1985 a) *Graded Assessments News-sheet No. 3*, University of London Schools Examinations Board.

—— (1985 b) *Graded Assessment in English Newsletter No. 1*, University of London School Examinations Board.

—— (1985 c) 'Levels of attainment in graded assessment schemes and other new forms of assessment and links with GCSE', Paper presented at a conference on Records of Achievement: Practical Issues, at Manchester University, January 1985, by the University of London School Examinations Board.

UTLEY, D., MITCHELL, R. and PHILLIPS, J.A. (1983) *Hear/say: a review of oral/aural graded tests*, Schools Council Examinations Bulletin 44, London: Methuen Educational.

VAN EK, J.A. (1977) *The Threshold Level for Modern Language Learning in Schools*, Council of Europe, London: Longmans.

WJEC (1985) 'Levels of attainment in graded assessment schemes and other new forms of assessment and links with GCSE', Paper presented at a conference on Records of Achievement: Practical Issues, at Manchester University, January 1985, by the Welsh Joint Education Committee.

WALKER, R. (1974) 'The conduct of educational case study: ethics, theory and procedures', in B. Macdonald and R. Walker (eds) *SAFARI: Innovation, Evaluation, Research and the Problem of Control. Some Interim Papers*, Centre for Applied Research in Education, University of East Anglia.

WARNOCK, M. (1985) 'A secondary revolution', *Illustrated London News*. September 1985, p. 27.

WARWICK, D. (1987) *The Modular Curriculum*, Oxford: Basil Blackwell.

WEST SUSSEX (1981) GOALS document F/1/Admin. Chichester: West Sussex County Council.

—— (1982) GOALS document F/2/Oral. Chichester: West Sussex County Council.

WILLMOTT, A.S. and HALL, C.G.W. (1975) O *level examined: the effect of question choice*, Schools Council Research Studies, London: Macmillan.

WITHERS, G. and CORNISH, G. (1984) *Assessment in practice: competitive or non-competitive*, Occasional Paper no. 11, Victorian Institute of Secondary Education, Melbourne.

Skill Descriptions on GOALS Certificates

(a) Level 1

At Level 1 of the West Sussex GOALS Scheme candidates must show that they are able to cope successfully in French with the listening, speaking and (recognition) reading needed to:

make personal contact with a French speaking person,
give simple information about themselves,
obtain similar information in return
ask the way and understand directions,
shop for food, gifts, stamps, etc.,
buy food and drink in a café,
express basic personal needs,
enquire about and express simple feelings and attitudes.

They should also understand something of the French 'background' to the topic areas listed above.

To gain the Level 1 Certificate, candidates must pass separate tests of speaking, listening and reading/background knowledge, scoring at least 50 per cent on each test.

(b) Level 4

At level 4 of the West Sussex GOALS scheme, candidates must show that they are able to cope successfully in French with the listening, speaking and reading needed to initiate and maintain a straightforward conversational exchange, and to process related spoken or printed material on the following subjects, which together make up the topic areas specified for the Council of Europe 'Threshold' Level. A test of letter-writing on one or more of these themes is a compulsory part of the examination (15 per cent).

1. Personal identification
2. Family and daily routine
3. Relations with other people, clubs and societies
4. House and home/accommodation
5. Local environment
6. Free time/leisure interests/holidays and entertainment
7. School routine/education/and career plans
8. Language
9. Shopping
10. Food and drink/café-restaurant
11. Public and emergency servies
12. Personal needs/health and welfare/dealing with accidents
13. Public transport/holiday travel
14. Weather

Candidates should also understand something of the French background to the topic areas listed above.

NB The Level 4 syllabus and tests have been accepted as a Mode III CSE examination by the Southern Regional Examinations Board (from summer 1983) for those pupils of the relevant age group whose entry is accepted by the Board via an approved centre, in accordance with SREB Regulations. The issue of this certificate is, however, totally independent of any public examination award, and should not be construed as necessarily conferring CSE equivalence.

Avon Science Certificate – Level 1 Criteria

(as listed on the back of the certificate)

Manipulative Skills

Good general manipulative skills are important. In addition, there are many skills related to unique pieces of science equipment that need to be clearly defined for that item of equipment alone. Many of these skills will have been taught

1 Assembly skills (a) assemble a 3D shape
                    (b) assemble an object from a series of components
2 Sorting skills: carry out sorting exercises requiring dexterity
3 Correct use   (a) use a small-size electric screw driver
                    (b) wire a mains plug (wire already cut and colours given)
                    (c) set up an electric circuit from a picture or photograph
4 Precision manipulative skills:
                   carry out an exercise requiring precision manipulation (for example use dropping teat pipette, tuning potentiometer so a meter reads precise number, measuring cylinder)
                   colour a diagram choosing colours and demonstrating control over area and shading
5 Correct use of basic science equipment
                    (a) use of retort stand
                    (b) bunsen burner
                    (c) filter paper in a funnel

6 Transfer skills (a) transfer a material from mortar
                    (b) transfer hot liquid out of beaker
7 Cutting skills (a) simple cut of biological specimen
                   (b) cut 2D shape from paper or card

Recording Skills

Every pupil should be able to

1. draw diagrams (with labels) of familiar, individual items of equipment.
2. identify items of equipment;
3. draw diagram of simple 'photo reduced geometric shape as viewed through a microscope (minimum × 40);
4. tabulate a given set of results with one column of results already completed;
5. answer simple questions given a drawn pie-chart;
6. construct a bar chart from a set of figures with both axes already labelled;
7. record results of experimental investigation on sheets provided.

Observational Skills

Observational skills inevitably imply elements of interpretational skills, the two being inseparable. There is also a strong link with recording skills, though here the two can be separated. The pupil should be able to

1. observe, identify and classify substances into one of three basic states of matter, describing changes of colour and state;
2. observe the colour of substances and match them to reference colour;
3. observe and interpret a range of instructional symbols, codes and letters relating to function and/or use;
4. observe and relate apparatus assemblies, components and specimens to drawn representation of them;
5. observe and identify potential hazards in school and everyday life;
6. demonstrate careful listening and watching of audio visual material.

Measurement Skills

Each pupil should be able to

1. make measurements of mass to an accurracy of 1 scale division;
2. measure lengths under a metre to the nearest mm;
3. measure lengths over a metre to ±1 per cent using a ruler or measure too short for the task;
4. use a stop clock to an accuracy of 1 second;
5. read volume in a measuring cylinder to 1 scale division;
6. measure + and − values of temperature to nearest scale division;
7. read an analogue meter to the nearest scale division (10 divisions).

Index